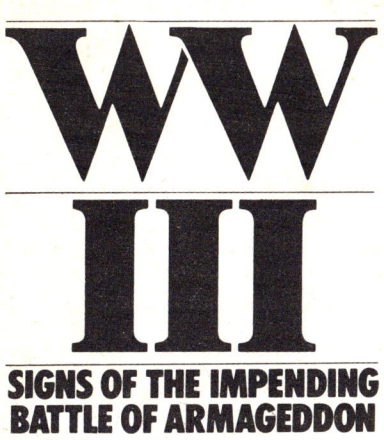

WW III

SIGNS OF THE IMPENDING BATTLE OF ARMAGEDDON

John Wesley White
WW III

SIGNS OF THE IMPENDING BATTLE OF ARMAGEDDON

REVISED EDITION

ZONDERVAN PUBLISHING HOUSE

OF THE ZONDERVAN CORPORATION | GRAND RAPIDS, MICHIGAN 49506

WW III
Copyright © 1977, 1981 by The Zondervan Corporation
Grand Rapids, Michigan

Library of Congress Cataloging in Publication Data
White, John Wesley.
  WW III.
  1. Bible—Prophecies—World War III.   I. Title.
BS649.W67W47   236   76-44820

Thirteenth printing
ISBN 0-310-34372-0

All rights reserved. No part of this publication may be reproduced, stored in a retrieval system, or transmitted in any form or any means—electronic, mechanical, photocopy, recording, or otherwise—except for brief quotations in printed reviews, without the prior permission of the copyright owner.

Printed in the United States of America

Contents

Foreword by Billy Graham / 7
Preface / 11
  1 The Apocalyptical Signs / 13
  2 The Physical Signs / 21
  3 The Technological Signs / 30
  4 The Astrophysical Signs / 41
  5 The Geophysical Signs / 49
  6 The Ecological Signs / 57
  7 The Biological Signs / 70
  8 The Economical Signs / 80
  9 The Sociological Signs / 91
10 The Criminological Signs / 101
11 The Psychiatrical Signs / 110
12 The Psychical Signs / 119
13 The Cosmological Signs / 130
14 The Philosophical Signs / 136
15 The Ecclesiastical Signs / 146
16 The Historical Signs / 158
17 The Political Signs / 173
18 The Christological Signs / 185
19 The Psychological Signs / 201

Foreword

"Super Bowl: Welcome to World War III" flashes a sports-page headline in a leading metropolitan daily! It is very well understood as the ultimate in gamesmanship! But World War III as a terrible, impending reality, looming ominously on the human horizon for people the world over, is something else! It spells the awesome prospect of consummation events, of universal holocaust, of apocalypse, of Armageddon. It issues in a claustrophobic feeling of helpless inescapability, of hopeless inevitability. It currently characterizes the writings of an Andrei Sakharov, an Aleksandr Solzhenitsyn, and figured in the later writings of the now-deceased Arnold Toynbee, Albert Schweitzer, and Albert Einstein. Whether you're reading the literature of diagnosis or prognosis, it seems that in the frightening world of today as the syndicated pundit Jack McArthur puts it, you encounter "almost solid gloom and disaster."

This is not to imply that we are not, as the Scriptures exhort, to pray for peace, seek peace, pursue peace, hope for peace. Jesus said, "Blessed are the peacemakers!" So as another New Year rings in to the sound of the peace bell, aspirations emitting from Buckingham Palace, from the

Vatican, from the Kremlin, from the Heavenly Gate in Peking, and from the White House in Washington, we are to join in the effort in the words of the Pope: "Peace, . . . we must want it at any cost!"

On the other hand, Jesus, who bade us be peacemakers, foresaw that before He returns as the Prince of Peace to set up His reign of universal peace and prosperity, human society will stagger like a drunkard back to his bottle—into the juggernaut of the worst war in history. It will begin with "rumors of wars"—that is, war talk, war preparations, and warmongerings. This will develop into wars of nations rising up against nations, and this in turn will escalate into the involvement of whole blocs of nations—kingdoms against kingdoms. All of this will plunge the world to its nadir—the war of all time, which will universally involve all mankind in a holocaust more horrendous than anything man has experienced since his appearance on this planet. With humanity locked irretrievably into Armageddon, with sure annihilation beckoning, Christ will suddenly come and miraculously save man from himself, and set up His kingdom throughout the whole world.

Good men throughout the ages have tried admirably to avoid an impending Armageddon. The great Jewish scholar, Rabbi Reuben Slonim, notes incisively that that for centuries organized religion has sincerely "promised to abolish war, establish the equality of all men, prohibit the exploitation of human beings, and transform the City of Man into the City of God. Despite the collective efforts of all cults and creeds, the sword is still a sword, not a ploughshare."

Jesus assured us that before the sword becomes a ploughshare, man would unsheath history's biggest and sharpest sword in the most woeful war of the ages. With 600 billion dollars being earmarked this year for weaponry, armaments, and death machines, Rabbi Slonim's point is well made.

In the past two generations, society has gone full circle. The bells that rang in the twentieth century resounded with optimism. Man had at last come of age. He was climbing right back over the fence, striding past the flaming cherubim and into the Garden of Eden again. The prophets to whom he chose to listen wore rose-tinted glasses and swore that Utopia was, with assists from the new technology and psychological sciences, within his grasp. He would soon rise far beyond the indignity of sweating to earn his bread, or shedding the blood of his fellows. He would so flourish and flower that the fragrance of his blossoming would perfume any lingering odors from his foul-scented past. Anyone who thought otherwise was considered an intellectual simpleton.

But alas! Two holocausts exploded over the earth and were called world wars. They wreaked more savagery and slaughter and wasted more people and property than the previous thousand years combined. As man looked up from the ashes, through the smoke, he could see that this time the flaming cherubim over Eden were thermonuclear signaling the fact that man would never vault himself over the fence back into the Garden. It was indeed Paradise lost! John Quincy Adams revealed his aspirations when he said, "I studied politics and war that my sons might study mathematics and philosophy, so that their children will study art." That all sounded like a very romantic dream, but it was a secular humanism that was to evaporate eventually into the stark realities of a Joan Baez lamentation to her leftist followers: "You are the orphans in an age of no tomorrows"; or of a retiring Henry Kissinger conceding that once "utopia was seen, not as a dream, but as our logical destination if we only traveled the right road." Alas! We've discovered "that the road is endless, that in traveling it we will not find utopia but ourselves." The prodigal son also came to himself, and in so doing he traveled the road that led him home.

Today as man finds himself in his own misery, he should be looking toward home. "Everybody would like to think that a god is going to come out of somewhere and lead us out of our troubles," said the Chairman of the Democratic National Committee on television. The fact of the matter is that God's Son is going to come back from heaven and fulfill His disciples' prayer through the ages: "Thy kingdom come. Thy will be done on earth as it is in heaven." The apostle Paul defined a Christian as one who has "turned to God from idols to serve the true and living God and to wait for His Son from heaven."

Meanwhile, Jesus instructed us to "discern the signs of the times." In *WW III*, John Wesley White isolates and identifies the signs that Jesus said would provide the world scenario signifying His impending return. He does so by taking the biblical prophecies that scholars for centuries have recognized as sure precursors of Christ's second coming. He parallels these with a careful scrutiny of current events and demonstrates thereby that we could very well be living close—very close indeed—to what the Bible calls the "time of the end."

To those of you who are Christians, I hope that a reading of this book will arouse you, in the words of the ancient prophet Joel, to "put ye in the sickle, for the harvest is ripe: come, get you down; for the press is full. . . . Multitudes, multitudes in the valley of decision: for the day of the Lord is near in the valley of decision." Let's go out and preach the gospel of the kingdom, as Jesus exhorted, and "then shall the end come." If you are not a Christian, my prayer is that your reading this book will cause you to "prepare to meet your God." Remember God's promise: "Whosoever shall call upon the name of the Lord shall be saved."

BILLY GRAHAM
Montreat, North Carolina

Preface

"We stand on the brink of what may be Armageddon," declares Billy Graham in Albert Hall, London, early in 1981, and Paul Harvey responds across America that this theme seems to obsess the great minds of our time. I hear Tom Landry, coach of the Dallas Cowboys, wonder out loud if Armageddon will be fought in the 1980s. The Canadian Department of National Defense polls our people and discovers a majority expect nuclear war will strike during this decade. Pope John Paul III didn't know when, but in an address to the United Nations, he warns: "Sometime! Somewhere! Somehow! Someone may well get his finger on the nuclear trigger." Rabbi Abraham Feinberg sees our world "teetering on a knife edge toward annihilation."

Americans generally, according to a polling in *Time* (February 1981), feel the gloom of doomsday: In 1977, 47 percent were optimistic of the future; in 1981, it's down to 18 percent. SALT negotiator Paul Warnke pleads before five thousand delegates to the American Association for the Advancement of Science meeting in Toronto in 1981 that "the bottom line is 'Co-existence or No Existence.'" The Bulletin of Atomic Scientists indicates that the Scientists themselves are not hopeful. In 1980, they moved their Doomsday Minute Hand up to 7 minutes to 12, in 1981, to 4 minutes to midnight!

WW III is neither pleasant writing nor pleasant reading—except for the Word of God: "For yet a little while, and he that shall come will come, and will not tarry" (Hebrews 10:37).

JOHN WESLEY WHITE
Toronto, Canada
February 1981

1

THE APOCALYPTICAL SIGNS

It was a chilly January day in 1981, when fifty-two released American hostages arrived by bus at the White House in Washington to be greeted by President Ronald Reagan. But it was one of the warmest welcomes in the history of the Republic, as flowing tears and overflowing embraces characterized the official homecoming of the newly free! They had been: "Prisoners of War," as the President described them during their 444-day captivity in Iran. "When the Lord turned against the captivity of Zion," recited the President, "we were like them that dream. Then was our mouth filled with laughter and our tongue with singing: then said they among the heathen, the Lord hath done great things for them . . . whereof we are glad" (Ps. 126:1-3).

One of these days, there's going to be a much more marvelous airlift of released captives, rising by special redemption of Jesus Christ on the cross, "to meet the Lord in the air, and so shall we ever be with the Lord" (1 Thess. 4:17). And in the words of the choir which sang at President Reagan's inauguration, all of us as believers throughout the ages shall truly see "the glory of the coming of the Lord."

Meanwhile, here on earth "we ourselves groan within ourselves, waiting for the adoption, to wit, the redemption of our body. For we are saved by hope" (Rom. 8:23, 24).

But alas for the present. Jesus alerted us, "You will hear of wars and rumors of wars. . . . Nation will rise against nation, and kingdom against kingdom." Our Lord was replying to His disciples' question: "What will be the sign of your coming and of the end of the age?" (Matt. 24:3,6,7). Continuing His answer to the apostle John a half century later, Jesus enlarged on how human warmongering would escalate into worldwide war incited by the "spirits of demons performing miraculous signs," driving blindly the heads of state "of the whole world, to gather them for the battle on the great day of God Almighty . . . to the place that in Hebrew is called Armageddon" (Rev. 16:14,16). That will indeed be World War III. WW I was fought in Western Europe. WW II enveloped three of the world's five continents and three of its five oceans. Armageddon will involve the nations "of the whole world," and as such will indeed be WW III. Its inciter and villain will be the Son of Perdition from hell, the Antichrist; its Savior and Victor will be the Son of God from heaven, Jesus Christ.

China's operational head Oeng Xiaoping, spokesman for the nation which has one-fifth of the world's population, reiterated in September, 1980 that mankind indisputably is headed for world war. "This is independent of man's will." Surely that has to be one of the most amazing statements in the annals of political atheism: that world war is "independent of man's will." It is precisely what Jesus assured John: that mankind would bottom out by falling into the hands of demonized rulers, who, with minds drugged and bewitched by Satan, would march him down the road to Armageddon. "It is too late to avoid the third World War," reckons Aleksandr Solzhenitsyn, as he witnesses the gladiatorial beating of war drums and immolational battle cries from Moscow to Washington, to Southeast Asia, to the Middle East, to Angola, to Rhodesia. The editor of Canada's leading news magazine was asked what is his chief worry. His reply: "Just what every other news magazine editor worries about—World War III being declared."

STATESMEN THE WORLD OVER ARE WORRIED

As we read chapters 38 and 39 of Ezekiel's prophecy, we cannot escape feeling that the prime mover of a major war en route to Armageddon is to be Soviet Russia. Leonid Brezhnev himself departs far enough from his usual chronic detente propaganda in 1980 to warn that only an "accident" or "miscalculation" stands between man and oblivion. On another occasion he "pleads" with the West not to "return to the Cold War and to an ever more risky balance on the brink of a hot war. . . . It is important for all to understand this well." One who believes he understands it well, exceedingly well, is British Tory Winston Churchill II, who replies wryly to Brezhnev:

> There is a nation whose armies—wherever they face the West—are always in attack formation. They are backed by an armaments industry consuming the same percentage of national wealth that Adolf Hitler spent one year before he plunged humanity into World War II. The nation is Soviet Russia. . . . Their whole economy is geared to a war footing.

Clare Booth Luce called herself "an optimist who thinks good things can happen but probably won't." She further states, "There is a great likelihood of nuclear war in the next twenty-five years."

United States Senator Robert Griffin, appearing on "Meet the Press," states that the world is sitting on a tinderbox with annihilation beckoning, while Senator Peter Dominick bemoans the fact that the only international agency that for a full generation has been in a position to negotiate peace is now in a state of strangulation: "We must frankly face the fact that the U. N., dominated by the General Assembly, no longer offers any hope or promise of peace."

Perhaps the most patrician premier on the planet is President Valery Giscard d'Estaing of France who reckons,

"The world is unhappy. It is unhappy because it doesn't know where it is going and because it senses that, if it knew, it would discover that it was heading for disaster." Henry Kissinger burst into tears before a television camera, as he stood in the Armageddon-bound Middle East, which had hanging over it an unmistakable thermonuclear sword-of-Damocles. Kissinger grieved, "One has to live with a sense of the inevitability of tragedy." Albert Sweitzer analyzed humanity's proclivity for self-destruction: "Man has lost the capacity to foresee and to forestall. He will end by destroying the earth."

WRITERS ARE CONVINCED THAT IT IS THE END

H. G. Wells witnessed man entering the nuclear age and articulated the fact that "For man and his world, there is no way out." Arnold Toynbee foresaw that as man enters the final years of this century, "people are going to find themselves in a permanent state of siege. . . . The future austerity will be perennial and it will become progressively more severe. What then?" And it is with this "What then?" that man senses apocalypse. *Time* points out that George Orwell's ominous prognostications a generation ago have made him today an uncanny "cliche for apocalypse." Or, as Clive Cooking writes: "We are currently entering the zone of 'Way stations of the Apocalypse.' " Best-seller books currently carry such titles as *Ultimatus* and *Doomsday*, an ubiquitous number engaging the catchword "Armageddon," such as *Armageddon, The Voice of Armageddon, The Road to Armageddon* and Billy Graham's *Till Armageddon*.

SCIENTISTS THEMSELVES ARE THE MOST ALARMED

Scientists have said for years that their biggest frustration is that over half of their research worldwide is spent on armaments: the invention of new engines for annihilation.

Flora Lewis of the *New York Times* reflects the thinking of nuclear "scientists who are projecting the future, usually in apocalyptic thunderclaps." Writing about the Science and Disarmanent Conference assembled in Paris, in 1981, she solemnized that the biggest threat of nuclear annihilation comes from the terrible possibility of "miscalculation." Andrei Sakharov, father of the Russian H-bomb warns that "the unchecked growth of thermonuclear arsenals and the buildup toward confrontation threaten mankind with the death of civilization and physical annihilation."

Perhaps his most influential collaborators in the West in the matter of man's perch on the precipice of self-extermination were the 2,300 American scientists calling themselves the "Union of Concerned Scientists," who presented a petition to the president of the United States. They included eight Nobel laureates and, what was most significant, "four scientists who held key positions in developing the first atomic bomb." They apprised the president of the "grave potential hazards" posed by nuclear energy, which, if "used in anger, . . . can create worldwide devastation."

One of the most distinguished watchdog bodies in the world is the Club of Rome. Including such members as Pierre Elliot Trudeau of Canada and several European heads of state, their study, entitled "Mankind at the Turning Point," warns that man is on a collision course with destruction: "The course which the world is presently following leads straight to catastrophe," adding that shortly "ten million children a year will die of starvation in Asia; 24,000 nuclear power stations will be spread around [the world with] all the potential for illicit bomb manufacture and for devastation caused by dumping of radioactive waste."

The world wire services carry the assessment of George Rathjens, Professor of Technology at Massachusetts Institute of Technology. Published initially in the *Harvard Magazine*, the distinguished scholar collaborating with four other MIT-Harvard experts, adjudged that man can expect a nuclear war in the next twenty years—probably being triggered by one of the smaller nations and spreading through the world. The concensus of this braintrust was that the only inhibiting force to make such a portentious holocaust unlikely would be "a very nasty kind of world government." So it boils down to this: Will the arms race, or the race towards a dictatorship over the whole human race, win out, or will both combine to do man in? Man is saddled with an inexorable time bomb. The fangs of impending extermination are penetrating toward his jugular. The minute hand on the atomic time clock is moving inevitably toward midnight. Man is obsessed with an ominous feeling that he is looking into the open end of a loaded cannon about to go off, with the same sick compulsion that attracts moths into a lethal flame. His is a death wish.

The movie moguls exploit and intensify this human apprehension to the hilt. Marlon Brando is featured in *Apocalypse Now*, and another title flashing on marquees around the world tom-toms *America Hurtling Toward Apocalypse*. The brilliant Oxford-trained playwright, Susan Sontag, was being interviewed by Jack Kroll, the senior editor of *Newsweek*, on CBS-TV. Asked what the dominant theme of films worldwide is, Sontag replied, "Apocalypse," adding that the younger and the farther to the left the playwright, the more "Apocalypse" dominated their thinking.

With the ominous threat of the total devastation of the environment and the decimation of life throughout the earth hanging over man, the media, it seems, is capable of communicating very little good news. Toronto pundit, Dennis Braithewaite laments, "The news today is just too awful to bear scrutiny." Bemoans Walter Cronkite, "Many times, I'd rather be a-song-and-dance man bringing some levity to you, instead of wrack and ruin. But we are on the threshold." Tom Alderman adds his comments in the *Canadian Magazine*, saying that the world scene is characterized by "massacres, fires, earthquakes, riots in the streets, the collapse of the world economy, the decline of political morality, the menace of bubonic plague, the erosion of the ozone layer . . . [and] Armageddon coming!"

Alderman says, "Not since the fallout-shelter scare of the late 1950s has there been such persistent talk of disaster, collapse, breakdown." He reveals that many Canadians are "looking for an apocalypse [and] are seeking, finding, building and stocking hideaways in the mountains or outbacks of our country." The *Winnipeg Free Press* carried an article on what it called a landslide toward yogis, gurus, and eastern-styled christs who are selling to frightened North Americans things like "5,000-dollar caves in the Himalayas" that ensure peace and safety to affluent malcontents. Richard Nixon tells how he was introduced in China to a whole underground network of survival tunnels, which the Chinese were convinced will be required for future refuge in a thermonuclear war.

This is scarcely idle speculation. Representative Les Aspin, a Wisconsin Democrat, describes how the American Pentagon spent 142.2 million dollars to hollow out of the Rocky Mountains in Colorado a headquarters for the North American Defense Command.

So we turn to a feature article in a national magazine and read of an enterprising young Californian, the son of a medical doctor, who makes a living by helping people plan their escape from a North American society that he flatly predicts will crumble in the near future. One of his clients, a former computer consultant who feels American civilization is doomed, has dug a hole six feet wide, eight feet high, and sixteen feet long in a national forest in Oregon. Under cover of winter, when forest rangers tend not to wander far from their quarters, this scientist burrowed like a badger. Now, with his wife and children, he lives in this hole. It is camouflaged so cleverly that a normal person could walk over it without being aware that it was there.

Another client is a millionaire dude rancher who spent $500,000 to go underground. He maintains a staff of twelve people and has a workshop to repair anything from firearms to farm tools and livestock for dairy products and meat—in short, everything necessary for a long stretch of self-sufficiency for several determined people.

People who believe this are the Mormons. Delos Ellsworth, director of The Ezra Taft Benson Agriculture Institute of Brigham Young University, is spear-heading a scheme for all Mormon households to stash away a year's store of food and other supplies in their basements—in case of "a war, an earthquake, a flood, a volcanic eruption," or some other "crisis."

All of this sounds rather bizarre! But it's an omen of things to come, when, as we read in the Revelation of Jesus Christ, man gets trapped in a holocaust of cascading calamities, and terrifying woes. Man will be so convulsed with fear that he has nowhere else to go: "The Kings of the earth, the princes, the generals, the rich, the mighty, and every slave and every free man hid in caves and among the rocks of the mountains. They called to the mountains and the rocks, 'Fall on us and hide us from the face of him who sits on the throne and from the wrath of the Lamb! For the great day of this wrath has come, and who can stand?' " (Rev. 6:15–17).

2

THE PHYSICAL SIGNS

A generation ago, when I dedicated my life to Christ at the age of fifteen and felt the compelling urge to go out and personally share my faith, the first person I confronted was an articulate agnostic. He was a militant antagonist of biblical Christianity. Dramatically seizing my Bible from my hand, he opened it with obvious practiced pomposity to 2 Peter 3:10,11 and, with curled lip and sardonic eye, read aloud these words: "The day of the Lord will come as a thief in the night; in the which . . . the elements shall melt with fervent heat, the earth also and the works that are therein shall be burned up" (2 Peter 3:10 KJV). Clapping the Bible shut and giving a sideways gladiatorial glance at his approving gallery, he left me quite dumbfounded and humiliated as he needled, "Sonny, don't you know that the only kind of fire is oxidation, and it doesn't remotely resemble that kind of destruction? When you can show me some fire of that kind, call me back and perhaps I'll become 'saved'!"

There seemed nothing else for me, a silenced awkward teenager, to say! Nothing, that is, for twenty-three months! Then one ominous summer morning in 1945, the world arose to confront the terrifying news that the first atomic bomb had been detonated—and mankind was pushed to the edge of a perilous precipice. Now man suddenly and against his will had a horrifying nuclear "Sword of Damocles" hanging over him. The scientist who led that first detonation team exclaimed, "I have just come back from the gates of hell!" Within thirteen years, Nikita Khrushchev would be saber-rattling his fifteen-megaton H-bomb, which, he claimed, when detonated, achieved a heat two and one half times as hot as the center of the sun, and which, in one explosion, had unleashed five times as much destructive power as all the weaponry of World War II combined. That was in the 1950s.

Looking into the 1980s the British journalist-historian, Alistair Cooke states, "I'll be astounded if this planet is still going fifty years from now. I don't think we will reach 2000. It would be miraculous!" The late Lord Mountbatten, as he lectured North Americans, said, "The Third World War" will surely be "fought with nuclear weapons." These statements were looked upon by many as just two more ringings of the doomsday bell. But when news leaked out that during the Yom Kippur War of 1973, when the Israelis were being backed into a corner, they had hastily assembled thirteen atomic bombs and actually "rushed them off to waiting air force units" (*Time*), it suddenly struck an all-too-complacent world how close to WW III man is.

Just how much warrant is there in the Scriptures for the probable use of thermonuclear weaponry? It has been pointed out by scholars that the Greek word *ouranoi* is the word from which our modern term *uranium* is derived. This white, radioactive metallic element possesses the uranium isotope U^{235} with its property for sustaining chain reaction and, therefore, is the basis for thermonuclear explosions, whether they be on the surface of the sun or right here on our planet.

So when we read again those words of Jesus that at the time of His return "the powers of the heavens (*ouranoi*) shall be shaken" (Matt. 24:29 KJV), that statement takes on the possibility of an interpretation different from what we understood it to have a generation ago. Does it refer to thermonuclear explosions? Perhaps. The probability is strengthened when we turn to 2 Peter 3:7 and read that by God's Word "the present heavens [*ouranoi*] and earth are reserved for fire." From this we may assume that it will be the same kind of fire that destroys both the earth and the heavens. Certainly verse 10 seems further to substantiate this position, for we read there that "the elements shall melt with fervent heat" (KJV).

Unpleasant but fearfully relevant reading is provided in many other passages of Scripture. In Zechariah, where so much prophecy is found, we read, "Behold the day of the Lord cometh . . . the Lord will smite all the people that have fought against Jerusalem; their flesh shall consume away while they stand upon their feet, and their eyes shall consume away in their holes" (Zech. 14:1,12). Those who have studied the Nagasaki and Hiroshima destructions contend that this is a precise description of what happened to some of the victims of the August 1945 bombings. In Revelation 9:16ff. we read of a destruction throughout the earth prior to the revelation of Christ, in which "a third of mankind was killed by the three plagues of fire." Prior to this, a "third of the trees were burned up" (8:7); "a third of the sea . . . a third of the living creatures in the sea died, and a third of the ships were destroyed" (8:8,9). Then there was another terrible conflagration: "a great star blazing like a torch, fell from the sky on a third of the rivers and on the springs of water . . . and many people died" (8:10,11). Again, in Revelation 16:8,9, we read of the release from above of "power to scorch people with fire. They were seared by the intense heat." Is it any wonder, really, that Jesus, in His allusion to those terrible times of holocaust on earth assured His followers: "For there will be great distress, unequaled from the beginning of the world until now—and never to be equaled again. If those days had not been cut short, no one would survive, but for the sake of the elect those days will be shortened" (Matt. 24:21,22). So when it is asked whether man—all people—will perish in a thermonuclear exchange between the super powers, or in a thermonuclear chain reaction, the answer is no. Christ will intervene, just before it would happen.

But, we read, a third of the population of the earth will disappear in one of these apocalyptic "fires." It is significant that the *Vancouver Sun* ran an article that begins, "Ottawa—Emergency planners say that up to eight million Canadians could be killed or injured in a large-scale nuclear attack on Canada." Eight million is a third of the population of Canada.

Just how close are we, physically, to this kind of destruction on the planet Earth, not in terms of potentially manufacturable nuclear weaponry, but of already stockpiled nuclear bombs? It is, of course, the business of the experts to keep this knowledge classified. But we can piece together some kind of picture that signifies how much nearer the world is to Armageddon than most people think!

Harvard biologist and Nobel Prize winner Professor George Wald reckons that there are, collectively, on this planet enough nuclear and thermonuclear warheads to equal ten tons of TNT for every man, woman, and child living today. There are at least six hydrogen bomb warheads being made every day. Physicist Alan Munn calculates that man could be obliterated from this world in two to three minutes. Andrei Sakharov, Russian scientist, warns, "The pulling of a few levers, the pushing of a few buttons, and the throwing of a few switches would result in the complete annihilation of every living thing on the earth." It is currently estimated that one hydrogen bomb, wrapped in cobalt and detonated in a strategic position, could exterminate three of the four and a half billion people currently populating this planet.

The most complete report that has been circulated to the general public on the current number of nuclear weapons in the American arsenal worldwide is one drawn up by Rear Admiral Gene R. La Rocque of the American Center for Defense Information in Washinton. Appearing in the *New York Times* it indicated that America possessed 30,000 nuclear weapons: 22,000 tactical and 8,000 strategic. Fifteen thousand of these are stored in the United States, at various stages of readiness for launching. The others include 7,000 in Europe, where, in cooperation with NATO, they are deployed for delivery aboard 2,250 aircraft, missile launchers, and nuclear cannons. The United States maintains 1,700 tactical nuclear weapons in South Korea and the Philippines and at United States installations on Guam and Midway in the Pacific. At sea, the United States has approximately 7,000 strategic and tactical nuclear weapons. Some 284 U.S. Navy ships and submarines are capable of delivering 12,000 tactical nuclear weapons in bombs, depth charges, torpedoes, and missiles.

As of this writing, it is estimated that the Soviets in one year have increased their nuclear stockpile 17 percent. Sir Peter Hill-Norton, Admiral of the British Fleet and Chairman of the NATO military committee reckons that as of now, the Russians are surpassing the Americans in nuclear stockpiling and delivery capacity, theirs being the advantage of secrecy. The American Joint Committee on Atomic Energy in Washington recently issued a warning that the Soviets have now overtaken the United States in nuclear striking power. They were gravely concerned over "the specter of a Soviet first-strike capability with a reserve second-strike capability."

Andrei Sakharov cautions that it is this "first-strike capability" that is so dangerous. He warns the West that "it is plain that the belligerent who unexpectedly delivers the first strike will be able, with 70 to 100 percent of his MIRV[1] missiles, to destroy immediately all of the enemy's launch sites, while with his remaining conventional missiles, he can destroy all of the enemy's cities, plus his military, industrial, and transport facilities and thus deal him a crushing blow, doing enough damage to decide the outcome of the war, without having been hit by a retaliatory strike. This is what is meant by 'the temptation of the first strike.'"

[1] Multiple Independently Targeted Reentry Vehicle.

Sakharov goes on to make the point that one of the areas where Soviet nuclear power is critically superior to that of the United States is in that their MIRV missiles have eight warheads, compared with three American warheads per missile.

The Carnegie Endowment for International Peace released in 1981 its detailed assessment of Soviet and American strategic nuclear strength. It pointed to the fact that whereas the U.S. has only 25 percent of its nuclear warheads in ICBMS, the Soviets have 75 percent of theirs!

Sakharov has no doubt, personally, that if the Soviets felt the timing was right, they wouldn't hesitate to obliterate the United States. NATO recently reported that the most alarming thing about the Soviets is that their whole military strategy is based on an offensive, rather than a defensive formation.

One thing, among others, that Henry Kissinger discovered during his visit to China was that the Chinese seem to have virtually total surveillance on the armaments arsenals of all the nations of the earth and know their locations. In the plainest of language, they avowed that the greatest concentration of nuclear weaponry in the world was in the Balkan area. And they emphasized three little words: "IT WILL MOVE!"

But what is even more foreboding to some is the spread of nuclear bombs to other smaller nations in the past few years.

It is generally estimated that India was able to detonate her first nuclear device because Canada sold her a nuclear reactor, allegedly for peaceful purposes. The *Washington Post* predicts that within two years, fifty-two countries will have nuclear reactors. How many of them will use these to develop their own nuclear bombs? Experts are divided on this, but even ths most optimistic observers are not prepared to project that the majority will not eventually use these reactors for purposes of weaponry, not peace.

Probably no area of international posturing is so fraught with hypocrisy as this matter of who possesses the nuclear device—at least, all the component parts—and who doesn't. It is inconceivable that if a Massachusetts Institute of Technology student could, in five weeks (222 hours), using published materials that can be found "in any good library," devise a nuclear bomb that, according to Dr. Jan Prawitz of the Swedish Defense Ministry would work, it simply is inconceivable that sophisticated countries like Japan, West Germany, Sweden, Argentina, Italy, or Iran could not assemble any reasonable number of thermonuclear weapons, if they judged their national interests called for them. Over and over again, the defense departments of the nations who have not publicly tested nuclear weapons, will avow they do not have a nuclear arsenal. What they usually mean is that they have never actually triggered a nuclear device, though all of the assembled components lie ready to bring together at a moment's notice.

One of the most frightening scenarios, of course is that in which Terrorists might use a nuclear device. As the Pentagon organ *Defense* (January 1981) noted: "More than a few specialists on terrorism have asserted that the day is fast approaching when an atomic bomb in the hands of a terrorist group will threaten to cover us all in a blanket of radioactive debris."

Biggest threat of such, of course, would come from the P.L.O. The Arabs, with their near monopoly of the oil export market, are in a unique position to buy outright—or even bribe—nuclear weapons from the "have" powers. President Qaddafi of Libya comments on the availability of atomic parts: "Soon the atom will have no secrets for anybody. Some years ago we could hardly procure a fighter squadron. Tomorrow we will be able to buy an atomic bomb and all its parts. The nuclear monopoly is about to be broken." The Russian Tass news agency refers to "Soviet-Libyan cooperation in the use of atomic energy."

Then there is the matter of the surplus of nuclear wastes accumulating from the normal peaceful uses of atomic power stations around the world. The Atomic

Energy Commission states that in 1980 the stockpile of atomic waste products in the United States alone was convertible into 4,000 bombs; by A.D. 2000, into 250,000 bombs. We've already noted that within two years an estimated fifty-two countries will be accumulating the stockpiles in lesser quantities.

So ominous is the nuclear threat against universal man today, that *Time* reckons that to terminate man's existence on planet Earth involves little more than a single "fluke or miscalculation." With the crash of a nuclear bomber, the FB-111 in Maine, the world was reminded again of how the human race is capriciously perched on the precipice of annihilation—if human judgment were to be the determining factor of man's survival.

Finally, it needs to be pointed out that there are other weapons in the laboratory hopper, if not in the actual stockpile of manufactured weaponry, with which man could do himself in. British scientists have had a good deal to say about the laser beam "death ray," which, mounted on aircraft and traveling out from its source at the speed of light, could melt anything on the surface of the ground within a seventy-five-mile range. In the authoritative *Jane's Weapons System* reference book on military hardware editor Ronald Pretty writes in the foreword, which is quoted around the world, that he feels the Russians and Americans have been in a fierce race to be first actually to perfect this "death-ray" monster. He reckons that both have already moved this weapon from the drawing board to the assembly line. "Beneath the guarded references to high-energy laser research and development in The American Department of Defense publications, and behind the Soviet silence on the subject, it is probable that these two powers are locked in a costly suprascientific struggle."

The American government is reportedly spending four billion dollars per year on automated weaponry, laser-beam development being the top item of priority. Already developed is a laser-beam "zap" gun, which emits a beam that can track a fighter plane, focus on it, and cut right through its surface to bring it down. In early 1981, the Americans for the first time actually tested this device.

Martin Luther once decried, "Cannons and firearms are cruel and damnable machines. I believe them to have been the direct suggestion of the devil. If Adam had seen in a vision the horrible instruments that his children were to invent, he would have died of grief." I wonder what Martin Luther would have thought if he had been alive in the last quarter of the twentieth century.

3

THE TECHNOLOGICAL SIGNS

James prophesied that "in the last days" there would be materialistic greed, perhaps amidst technological wonders, but it surely would incur the judgment of God before Christ returns to set up His kingdom. "You rich people," he exclaimed, "weep and wail because of the misery that is coming upon you. Your wealth has rotted, and moths have eaten your clothes. Your gold and silver are corroded. Their corrosion will testify against you and eat your flesh like fire" (James 5:1-3).

The West and the Middle East are especially rich today in the areas of science and technology. Physicist Allan Bromley of Yale, president of the American Association for the Advancement of Science, entitled its 1981 Conference "Science and Technology: Bridging the Frontiers." He described ours as the most exciting time in history for a scientist to be alive. *The Wall Street Journal* notes that it is an American "dream that technology can cure all ills." Colonel Frank Borman asserts, "I believe now that man can do anything he wants, technically." This attitude led Prince Phillip to refer to today's "high priests of science" in an address in which he called universal man to put his faith again in the God, who has provided us with all these good things. Otherwise, he said, they will turn and devour us. Whether man's scientific achievements of the twentieth century are chiefly retrogressional or progressional is currently one of man's monstrous dilemmas. Whether technology is to be man's elevator to Utopia or his annihilation to oblivion is the secularists' biggest bugaboo. The concluding resolution of the World Council of Churches, which met in Nairobi issued a timely warning that today's biggest blessing to many—scientific wonders—is also the biggest problem of our age. The resolution cited "technological 'giantism' and 'consummerism' as draining nature and depressing humanity." And so into the eighties, in both ecclesiastical and scientific conferences, whether at an assembly of the National Council of Churches or at an American Association for the Advancement of Science conference, the planners for a better world are debating and agonizing over this dilemma. Technology could offer man either "untold good" or "incalculable evil." Perhaps the sharpest controversy has been whether or not an energy-short world should turn to an immense, reproducible source of nuclear power—the by-product plutonium that can be multiplied even as it is used—to boost continuing economic growth and a richer society. That route involves the risk of more tragedies like Three Mile Island.

Tragedies could mean a "Faustian bargain," bioethics professor Margaret Maxey of the University of Detroit gravely warns, referring to the storied Faust who made a deal with the devil for temporary delights, eventuating in his doom. On the other hand, she reflected, it could provide an unprecedented spur to a "new level of cultural evolution," bringing acceptance of "the imposition of a global commitment to a permanent, stable, more just social order."

It would require a "technological paradise" of flawlessly arranged and universally heeded controls to prevent such expansion from poisoning the earth, states Nobel prize-winning physicist Hannes Alfren of the University of California. Harvard's biochemist John T. Edsall adds, "I'm unable to see such a degree of stability," for, in man's history, it "has never existed." What is amazing about these observations, is that this is precisely what will happen when Christ comes to diffuse World War III and set up His kingdom on this earth. His personal control will ensure it. Meanwhile, it is commendable that such conventions should be held, as, for example, the "Shaping the Future" conference of science and technology experts and theologians who gathered at Deep River, Ontario, to air their "scientific and Christian concern" over the direction the world of technology is going. But in the end, Christ's coming again is the only solution.

Let us clarify a question that has certainly arisen in my mind about this matter of technology. The question is this: Won't there be such apocalyptic holocaust and destruction in the future that technological research and scientific advances will be thwarted? No, for war has always produced pressures, fierce life-and-death rivalries that have caused scientific leaps forward that would not otherwise have occurred. I suspect that as many crucial scientific inventions were made during the six years of World War II as during the first forty years of this century, combined; e.g., the development of the jet airplane, the atomic bomb, radar, the purification of penicillin, and the launching of the age of antibiotics. The "deceiver," the Antichrist, will be a wonder-worker. Many of his "miracles" may be suddenly discovered or invented technologies that are used to impress the masses with his supposed, as well as his real, supernatural powers.

Meanwhile, James warned that "in the last days" materialism will threaten to "eat your flesh like fire." One of the technological wonders (dealt with in the last chapter) that threatens to turn this planet into an upstairs from perdition, if it's not the downstairs of paradise, is nuclear energy. As one pundit says: "Perhaps splitting the atom was not such a wise crack after all!" It would be wise if man could turn all of his energies toward constructive rather than destructive goals. Much government research has been invested in exploring the peaceful uses of atomic energy. The Geneva Conference alone has published thirty-three volumes on the peaceful use of atomic energy, while the American Chemical Society has published 40,000 pages, and the *Electronic Engineer* 32,000. *Time* goes so far as to reflect that nuclear power has to be thought of as "one of the best hopes for meeting United States energy needs in the last two decades of the century." A poll taken of the American people reveals that 60 percent approved of expanding nuclear power for peaceful uses.

But right here is the problem. Pierre Trudeau says that if man is to live at all, he must live "dangerously," and that includes taking the calculated risk of harnessing nuclear energy sources. The Club of Rome has had a great deal to say about the potential for man's destruction that there is in technology. On the other hand, the Club points up the fact that it is possible to "contend that all the crises of the present age are strictly technical" and that "technology" with a capital *T* like a fairy with a magic wand, "could" perform a new miracle. "In the realm of energy . . . in 50 years . . . nuclear energy will meet all our needs." Then the Club turned pessimistic again and reverted to the impending doom man faces, because he himself essentially is morally unreformed.

The Canadian Archbishop E. W. Scott, Moderator of the World Council of Churches, remarked on the dangers of nuclear energy that "the fantastic explosion of knowledge in the last two decades has brought more questions than answers. Man's problem today, ironically enough, is his knowledge. In the ancient Garden of Eden, when it was pointed out to Adam and Eve that their eating of the fruit of the tree of knowledge of good and evil would lead to death, they could not understand. And man from those ancient times until the mid-twentieth century could not understand. But we understand today. And part of the nostalgia of the eighties is for the safe days when man didn't have the "knowledge" of the nuclear device. A polling of the American people indicated that for this very reason the majority of people feel that the best days of life in the United States are past.

But the Bible does tell us that a knowledge explosion will occur at the time of the end (Dan. 12:4). The *Toronto Globe and Mail* editorializes that knowledge is currently doubling every ten years. In the realm of the furthering of technology, 75 percent of all the scientists of history are alive at this moment. There are 35,000 scientific journals being published and circulated in the world today. Dr. Malcolm Todd, President of the American Medical Association reckons "that about half of medical knowledge is outdated every ten years. If that is true, then a doctor who has not taken any postgraduate courses since he left medical school in, say, 1950 would really be practicing back in the Dark Ages." Seventy-five percent of the medicines in use today have been developed since World War II.

Many of the dramatic advances of science have been linked to the fact that universal education has been a goal of the peoples of the whole world, particularly in this generation. As Walter Pitman puts it, "The entire life-style of our society must be focused on education as a normal function throughout our lives." After the "hippy" revolt of the late sixties, which downplayed education, students are back, diligently studying again. Perhaps a look at Canada and, say, India will illustrate what has happened in a single generation. In Canada, there are seven times as many graduating from college or university today as there were in 1950. In India, since 1950 the number of college students increased from 330,000 to 3.8 million—up ten times. From the point of view of world literacy, the number of new books annually being published is escalating: 90,000 in the Soviet Union; 85,000 in the United States; 45,000 in West Germany; 35,000 each in Britain and Japan. The number of illiterates worldwide in the last fifteen years has dropped from 40 percent to 30 percent.

Enhancing this knowledge explosion are electronic devices that were not available to our fathers. There is the computer, a machine (acting more and more like a superman) that is barely a quarter of a century old. Today's computers are capable of incredible feats. The United States

Navy has developed a new "crosstie memory" computer that is capable of storing 70 million bits of information on every square inch of thin magnetic tape. A sophisticated computer can perform 60 billion transactions in one second. When Apollo XIII got lost in space, it would have taken a scientist over a million years to figure out with a pencil and paper a way to bring it back. Computers did it in less than an hour and a half. Computers can fly the Boeing 747 or Concorde jets with virtually no need for human assistance. Computers can also project into the future with an accuracy that is as uncanny as it is frightening. There is at the headquarters of the ECC in Belgium a computer called "the Beast." It is three stories high and, we are told, can number every one of the four and one half billion humans on the planet, retaining detailed information on his character, creditability, and beliefs. Ruth Davis, director of the National Bureau of Standards Institute for Computer Sciences and Technology, informs us that "the first battles of World War III may well have occurred when mathematical formulations of strategies and counter strategies of realistic proportions were able to be tried out as war games on computers."

Then there is television. When one of our children graduates from high school, he or she has spent as many as 17,000 hours watching television while spending 11,000 hours in school. Granted that much of this militates toward violence andeven intellectual superficiality, it also gives a student an overview of his world and a conception of his universe that earlier generations never had.

Are there hints in the Bible of the use of television in connection with the second advent of Christ? In 1981, there are a half a billion TV sets around the world, distributed more and more evenly among the 4.5 billion human beings. That is, there is one set for every ten people. And whether it's an American President in Peking, or the Olympics in Moscow, through the series of Telstar and other satellite systems, it's now possible for virtually the whole world to watch news as it happens. Technology, "noted Billy Graham in 1980, will "hasten the appearance of the

Antichrist, who will be seen worldwide on television." On the other hand, as Charles Taylor pointed out in 1981, TV videotape is made of ground stone. With the Gospel on television, the biblical assurance that the stones will cry out is surely fulfilled.

For nineteen centuries, Bible students simply could not make sense out of Revelation 11:9,10 where we read of the two witnesses who were to be killed in Jerusalem, where their Lord was crucified, and that "for three and a half days men from every people, tribe, language and nation will gaze on their bodies" and "the inhabitants of the earth will gloat over them and will celebrate by sending each other gifts." But television makes prophecies like this immediately credible. Even more dramatic will be the final Revelation of Jesus Christ, at the time of Armageddon when the world will exclaim, "Look, he is coming with clouds, and every eye will see him." The fact that television cameras have gone with men to the moon and we have felt we were only a few feet away from events there demonstrates what the potential of television is. Cameras have been set up on Mars, a place man himself cannot yet go, and on television sets in our living rooms, we've been looking around our solar system, seeing remarkably clear photographs of the Martian landscape.

Several satellite have been sent beyond the solar system to "look around" the adjacent constellations of stars.

This brings up the matter of the coming again of Jesus Christ and the matter of the judgment (or judgments). In 2 Timothy 4:1, we read, "In the presence of God and of Christ Jesus, who will judge the living and the dead, and in the view of his appearing and his kingdom, I give you this charge." Certainly God Almighty will not be restricted to minuscule camera and television equipment for His judgment, as we are; but when we can watch Senate hearings on the qualifications of a cabinet minister of a General Haig to be Secretary of State on international television, see every minute detail of facial expressions and body gesticulations, and hear barely audible mutterings, all in your home—

whether you're in Toronto, Chicago, London, Tokyo, or Sydney—you can, in some measure at least, conceptualize what the great judgments of God may be like.

The apostle Paul wrote that at Christ's coming "we must all appear before the judgment seat of Christ, that each one may receive what is due him for the things done while in the body, whether good or bad" (2 Cor. 5:10). Paul went further: he wrote that on the judgment day "God will judge men's secrets through Jesus Christ" (Rom. 2:16). Jesus Himself told us, "By thy words thou shalt be justified, and by thy words thou shalt be condemned" (Matt. 12:37 KJV). We have known, most of our lives, about recording words and playing them back on a phonograph or tape recorder. But electronics physicists are now telling us that the vibrations our words impress into, say, the rocks that surround us, could be extracted. Wouldn't it be amazing if Moses' words at the burning bush were extracted some day from the stones that surrounded him? The Bible tells us that it is possible for the stones to cry out!

Then there is the matter of God being a "human-heart watcher." The Bible does tell us that "man looketh on the outward appearance, but the Lord looketh on the heart" (1 Sam. 16:7). God says this. Man is now capable of looking out into the universe through a radio-telescope nearly two miles long in the Netherlands, or through one with a face a thousand feet in diameter in Puerto Rico, capable of spotting a postage stamp on the moon. If this is true, what can't Christ at His coming again see in the human heart when "nothing . . . is hidden from God's sight. Everything is uncovered and laid bare before the eyes of him to whom we must give account" (Heb. 4:13). The Chinese launched into orbit a series of sophisticated spy satellites from their Shuangchengtze missile complex at the edge of the Gobi Desert in Inner Mongolia. With these satellites they can monitor minute details of life in the Soviet Union and the United States in particular, and the rest of the world in general. Both Russia and the United States have a network of "spy-in-the-sky" satellites that on a clear day can allegedly count the number of potato hills in your garden, or even, when you are sitting on a lawn chair, read your newspaper over your shoulder. If man can do this with his current technology what can God do?

We are told in Daniel 12:4 that in "the time of the end" men will travel about, presumably with incredible speed. Ordinary transatlantic travelers can cross the Atlantic aboard the Concorde in two and a half hours today—about ten times as fast as Charles Lindbergh's famous flight a half century ago. Is air travel predicted in the Bible? Perhaps. We read in Isaiah 31:5 that "as birds flying" so will the Lord defend Jerusalem. No air force in the world is more agile than that of modern Israel.

In a book like this, which deals so largely with the ominous signs of woe and war that are to characterize the world scene at the time of the end of the age and the coming again of Christ, it might appear to a reader that the future of this world is one of unbroken gloom and doom. Nothing could be further from the truth. It is true that history's bleakest, blackest years are indeed those that lead to World War III. But that will be followed by the glorious thousand-year period of peace and prosperity that Jesus Christ will bring to this earth. Under His universal reign, humanity will rise to heights of happiness never before realized, or even dreamed of, in the history of man on this planet. It is my belief that with science and technology yielding such unprecedented progress today, unhampered by crime, war, and hate as they will be under the benevolent reign of Jesus, every invention will be utilized for man's freedom and fulfillment here on the earth—for a thousand years.

Stephen Rosen's *Future Facts*, a serious projection into the future of life on this planet, presupposing man's freedom from the hazards of his own depravity, depicts technology revolutionizing human existence beyond our fondest dreams. Dr. Rosen, whom the *New York Times* lauds as one of the most knowledgeable and responsible futurists in the world today, was trained in the astrophysics of cosmic radiation and was a research scientist at IBM and the Institute d'Astrophysique in Paris. Currently, he is a consultant on new products, services, and markets of the future to major foundations, *Fortune*-500 corporations, and other future-oriented firms.

Dr. Rosen sketches how a commuter will be able to take a twenty-one-minute subway ride from New York to Los Angeles in the morning and return in the evening. That's running "to and from," all right! And you will swallow a knowledge pill that teaches you Spanish—or any other subject. That's certainly an example of how "knowledge shall increase." And you will eat and drink food and beverages that have heated or chilled themselves in a matter of seconds.

In that day you could have breakfast that was cooked by sunlight, glide to the station in your plastic car, catch the flying train to the city, and be assured by your nuclear watch that you have time to stop off at your vacation submarine home to pick up the ski mini-tractor so you won't have to wait in a lift line when you take your lunch break. All of this may give you a headache, but you'll solve that by taking an electric aspirin.

Rosen cites advanced technology of today, which makes potentially possible not only the foregoing but also the following: a lightweight super flywheel that delivers 100,000 horsepower for three seconds, a nuclear-powered artificial heart, a man-powered plane, vaccines for cancer and meningitis, and a sure cure for the common cold. Video typewriters, super trees, paper stronger than steel, invisible planes, and injections that transmit memory and knowledge will also appear in the outreaching hand of man. And you will control your weight by electric brain-stimulation. Enzymes will keep you young indefinitely. Will man, indeed, live a thousand years, as Methusaleh almost did, and as implications indicate in Isaiah, Ezekiel, Zechariah, and Revelation that man will be capable of doing during the future millennium on this earth? Meanwhile in 1981, we're reading of the death of the oldest North

American, aged 113, and the oldest human being, 116. Until the seventies, there were many much older, including an American who lived to be 137. But alas, at the very time we're hearing of how science and technology are such boons to humanity, man seems to be unable to extend his life. Only Christ has the gift of eternal life. For all who are His, He is coming again—to receive us home, and so shall we ever be with the Lord.

4

THE ASTROPHYSICAL SIGNS

Man has always longed to fly and eventually to ascend into space. In this last third of the twentieth century, man is not only flying billions of miles per year, he is ascending, not fictionally, but factually to the skies in a Columbia onto the moon, and soon, he speculates, to Mars.

What is behind man's willingness to expend 150 billion dollars to buy a dozen round-trip tickets to the moon and perhaps a trillion dollars to get one man to Mars? On a TV network, one of those dozen, Charles Duke, was giving his testimony for Christ in 1981. He had been converted. John Schlesinger was quoted as saying that: "the Space Program marked the end of when man would feel at home on this earth." Probably the world's most prominent science-fictionist of our times is Ray Bradbury. On Walter Cronkite's CBS News, Bradbury reckons that there is no doubt about it: the motivation that spurs man on in the whole space-race craze is that he is obsessed with the irrepressible urge to make his home in the stars.

Unregenerate man has this universal urge, but he cannot define what it is. The Christian can. The apostle Paul wrote that "we know that if the earthly tent we live in is destroyed, we have a building from God, an eternal house in heaven, not built by human hands. Meanwhile we groan, longing to be clothed with our heavenly dwelling, since when we are clothed, we will not be found naked. For while we are in this tent, we groan and are burdened because we do not wish to be unclothed but to be clothed with our heavenly dwelling, so that what is mortal may be swallowed up by life. Now it is God who has made us for this very purpose and has given us the Spirit as a deposit, guaranteeing what is to come.

"Therefore we are always confident and know that as long as we are at home in the body we are away from the Lord. We live by faith, not by sight. We are confident, I say, and would prefer to be away from the body and at home with the Lord. So we make it our goal to please Him, whether we are at home in the body or away from it. For we must all appear before the judgment seat of Christ, that each one may receive what is due him for the things done while in the body, whether good or bad" (2 Cor. 5:1-10).

So we long to rise to be with Christ and, actually, "we will be with the Lord forever" (1 Thess. 5:18). That is true hope. "Hope," writes William Ellis in *Time*, is why we're sending the Columbia "migrating to a new frontier . . . the colonization of space." In the last twenty years a plethora of astrophysical possibilities has come to us on the crest of the space quest. For example, when the astronauts aboard the Apollo and the cosmonauts aboard the Russian Soyuz had their space rendezvous headlines around the world declared, "Americans and Russians Meet in Space." But they had to meet first on earth to prepare for the event. The Bible tells man, "Prepare to meet thy God" and then one day we who are Christ's will be caught up "to meet the Lord in the air" (1 Thess. 4:17). What a rendezvous that will be!

Another space-program analogy is that of the space suits required by the astronaut pioneers who went to the moon. They had to wear suits designed to the minutest detail to enable them to overcome the hazards of space travel. Any failure to meet exact and highly technical requirements in this realm, or a very slight departure or breakdown from precise requirements, would have resulted in the jeopardizing of the astronauts' lives. When Christ comes again, the first thing He will do is issue us glorified bodies like His. The apostle Paul taught, "Our citizenship is in heaven. And we eagerly await a Savior from there, the Lord Jesus Christ, who, by the power that enables Him to bring everything under His control, will transform our lowly bodies so that they will be like his glorious body" (Phil. 3:20,21). In 1 Corinthians 15:50-54, a favorite passage of Winston Churchill, Paul explained that this was "a mystery"; that is, it would take a special miracle: "We shall all be changed—in a flash, in the twinkling of an eye." This would be necessary because "flesh and blood cannot inherit the kingdom of God, nor does the perishable inherit the imperishable." So God performs this necessary miracle and "when the perishable has been clothed with the imperishable, and the mortal with immortality, then the saying that is written will come true: Death has been swallowed up in victory.'"

Something the space quest has demonstrated is that man can break away from the gravity of this planet and actually rise to the heavens. Centuries ago Jeremiah had written, "Behold the days come, saith the Lord" when men will "mount up to heaven" (Jer. 51:47,53).

In biblical times, in addition to our Lord's ascension, there was the ascension of Enoch, Elijah, and perhaps Paul—the apostle frankly stating that whether or not he was in the body, he couldn't say.

In the space program, scientists have learned how to hurl man in his craft aloft from the earth and into orbit, at a speed of 19,000 miles per hour, and then, to cause him to break out of orbit and out of the gravitational pull of the earth at 25,000 miles per hour, sending him into outer space a quarter of a million miles straight away from the world to the moon. In the airlift of the ages, all the saints of all generations and nations will rise to meet Christ and with Him ascend into heaven. What an event!

Another fact from the space race research findings that

is analogical to the return of Christ, is that the Bible says "that there should be time no longer" (Rev. 10:6 KJV). When those who believe in Christ are set free from time and space limitations and receive glorified bodies, time actually will become obsolete. In 1908, Albert Einstein suggested that as gravity weakened, time would run faster. Physicist Carrol Alley was able to demonstrate this recently. He remarked, "Einstein's predictions about time have been among the most controversial in modern physics." But today they're proved right. The curvature of time, though difficult to detect, creates the basic geometry of the universe." It is a well-publicized fact of the space-race program that were a man in a space ship able to travel at the speed of light—186,000 miles per second—time for him would cease. It has been predicted that by the end of this century, scientists, if their research progress is not impeded, will have man traveling at the speed of light. If he could do so, he would in fact terminate time. Eternity and infinity would merge and time per se would no longer exist.

What will propel glorified man aloft? In 1 Thessalonians 4:16, we read that "the Lord Himself will come down from heaven, with a loud command, with the voice of the archangel and with the trumpet call of God." There is a threefold sound: Christ's personal "loud command," "the voice of the archangel," and "the trumpet call of God" (1 Thess. 4:16). It is demonstrable in several laboratories of the world that by a sonic boom, a steel ball a foot in diameter can be lifted and held aloft indefinitely. Whether there is any relationship between these two points is not very important. It is of paramount importance, however, that we realize that God has any number of laws at His command to enact His will, and He could very well use the sonic boom or some similar phenomenon as a part of His resurrection and rapturing home of His own. Even so, it should be remembered that God is not bound by present laws of nature. The ascension of Christ was surely not associated with any loud sound.

This leads us to the statement of our Lord in Matthew 24:31, "And He will send His angels with a loud trumpet call, and they will gather His elect from the four winds, from one end of the heavens to the other." The problem this has always posed, however, is this: Could "His elect" be in the "heavens" and require gathering by angels at Christ's coming again? The answer of course is that many believers may well be in space at the time of the "second coming" of Christ. *Time* presented a feature article on "Colonizing Space," in which a plan is put forward for large numbers of people to move out to a gigantic space platform. The technology for living out there is already potentially developed. *Time* ran another article on the development of the shuttling of people back and forth to these living quarters in space. The development of the 5.25-billion-dollar project is already in effect with the launching of the Columbia, with plans for transporting passengers with the casualness of "today's businessmen" taking "the shuttle between Washington and New York." The Columbia (and its successors) will be able to be used at least a hundred times over. It is approximately the size of a DC-9.

As man heads into a time of great tribulation on this earth after the rapture, millions will seek a place to escape. Many perhaps will head out into space. So then when Christ comes at the time of His revelation, He will gather together all the extant saints of the earth, and, if this is the application, those in space. It is important to note that this does not refer to the rapture. If it did, it might imply that only if believers were in space—as, say, Jim Irwin was—would it be possible for Christ to come for His church. The New Testament is clear. Christ may come at any moment for His own to rapture them to heaven.

"And he will send his angels": When Christ comes, He is going to have angels deliver His saints to be forever with Him. Are we living at a time when angels are coming more and more out into the open? And are they not only appearing and speaking, but actually physically becoming involved in the affairs of man? When the Bible-believing Christian is confronted by questions like this, he or she should go directly to the Bible. What does the Bible say?

It has a great deal to say about angels. In fact, it declares that if people are knocking at your door and you go and find that they are strangers to you, you may well be about to entertain angels, unaware of the fact that you are doing so. The writer to the Hebrews exhorted, "Do not forget to entertain strangers, for by so doing some people have entertained angels without knowing it" (13:2).

Throughout Bible history, angels appeared to people, sometimes as people and sometimes in strange forms, postures, and even vehicles. They sometimes appeared in dreams, as they did to Joseph (Matt. 1:20; 2:13,19), or in visions, as they did to John (numerous references in the Book of Revelation). They often came by night as they did to Paul (Acts 27:23) and Peter (Acts 12:8). Sometimes they were dramatically dressed in brilliant white, had faces like lightning, and were generally so clothed with the glory of the Lord that they were overpowering (Matt. 28:2; Luke 2:9; Acts 1:10). They often were multiwinged (Isa. 6:2) or appeared as what we might label UFOs; e.g., among whirling wheels of magnificent splendor (Ezek. 10).

Frequently they appeared quite indistinguishable from human beings. When they were embodied, they were often, in appearance and in capacities for communication and achievement, very much like men. The apostle Paul wrote to the Corinthians that "the angels in heaven have bodies," which, though "different from ours," were nonetheless "bodies." A few verses later, he said, "Just as there are natural, human bodies, there are also supernatural, spiritual bodies." The celestial bodies of angels, unlike our terrestial bodies, are, as Paul points out, not subject as "our earthly bodies," to death and decay (1 Cor. 15:40,42,44). Yet on the surface they can look very much alike.

Angels are able to do many things, both humanlike and superhuman. They appear. They can eat a meal (Gen. 19:3; also see Heb. 13:2). They have desires (1 Peter 1:12). They give compliments (Judg. 6:12). They judge (Matt. 13:29,49). But they will not control the future world (Heb. 2:5). They can be seen by animals (Num. 22:23). They have many languages (1 Cor. 13:1). They can speak with a loud voice (Rev. 5:2) and blow a trumpet (Matt. 24:31). They are happy when sinners repent (Luke 15:10). They sing as a choir (Luke 2:13,14). They mobilize as a mighty army (Matt. 26:53). They can kill an individual (Acts 12:23) or a multitude of people, like, say, 185,000 (2 Kings 19:35) single-handedly, or a billion and more people (Rev. 9:15).

Thousands of years ago, two angels were instrumental in destroying the cities of Sodom and Gomorrah by triggering off a fire that seems to some observers to have been a nuclear explosion (Gen. 19:12-29). On the other hand, an angel can effect physical healings to human beings (John 5:4; Rev. 13:3,4). They can do such things as roll away a huge stone (Matt. 28:2), open prison gates (Acts 12:10), and undo chains (Acts 12:7). They can pull a threatened man through a door and lock out would-be intruders, temporarily blinding them (Gen. 19:10,11). So it does not seem at all out of character that when Christ comes again, angels should be delegated to gather Christ's elect together to be with Him.

Is there a link between the angel order of the universe, and some UFOs? Perhaps! Here in North America, 30 million people claim to have seen UFOs, and the numbers are dramatically on the increase, an actual majority of the total population now believing they exist. Dr. J. Allen Hynek, head of the Astronomy Department of Northwestern University in Chicago has investigated 777 reported UFO appearances. Four-fifths of them he dismisses as delusions of one kind or another, but he insisted that the other 20 percent merited serious investigation.

A poll report that 332 of 357 French people with the highest I.Q.s—that is 93 percent—believe in the likely existence of UFOs. The current popular interest in UFOs can be seen in the innumerable book titles appearing on this subject and the various TVserials (such as "Space 1999") that regularly feature this theme.

There are many mysteries attached to any attempt to link UFOs to the angelic order and the role they will play in the second coming of Christ. But there can be no doubt that there is an enormous surge of interest in these themes throughout today's world. On the other hand, the second coming of Christ can be ridiculously exploited by linking speculative and highly subjective ideas to it. For example, *Time* featured an account of between twenty-one and twenty-six Oregonians, in addition to people from California, New York, Nebraska, and Colorado, who have joined a cult known as "HIM" (Human Individual Metamorphosis). It is led by "the Two," who demand that their names not be disclosed, and that their disciples sign away everything they possess, apart from bare necessities, and follow them into their highly secretive colony. No one seems to be able to locate their community. "The Two" claim to have come from the same "Kingdom" as Jesus Christ. They say they will be assassinated sometime soon, rise from the dead in three and one-half days, and then leave for home in a UFO. They promise to take all of their followers with them in a UFO departure for a new and permanent home in the skies.

For such cultist exploitations of the second coming of Christ, Jesus gave us clear warning in His Word. In Matthew 24:23-28 we read:

> At that time, if anyone says to you, "Look, here is the Christ!" or "There he is!" do not believe it. For false Christs and false prophets will appear and perform great signs and miracles to deceive even the elect—if that were possible. See, I have told you ahead of time. So if anyone tells you, "There he is, out in the desert," do not go out; or, "Here he is, in the inner rooms," do not believe it. For as the lightning comes from the east and flashes to the west so will be the coming of the Son of Man. Wherever there is a carcass, there the vultures will gather.

"Prepare to meet thy God" (Amos 4:12). "Prepare" —that was a familiar word to astronauts John Young and Robert Crippen as they spent 1,600 hours in the Columbia. "Prepare" to meet Christ at His coming is the message of the Scriptures.

5

THE GEOPHYSICAL SIGNS

When Jesus' disciples asked Him, "What will happen to show that it is time for Your coming and the end of the age?" (Matt. 24:3 TEV), Jesus replied that among the signals will be "earthquakes in various places" (Matt. 24:7). *Time* tells us that there have been as many massively destructive earthquakes in the past twenty years as there were in the previous hundred. And there have been as many deaths in earthquakes—well over a million—in the last five years as there were in the first seventy-five years of this century. There were the Algerian and Italian earthquakes of 1980 which wiped out an estimated 23,000 lives. And John W. White, the author of Doubleday's new book *Pole Shift*, is predicting much bigger earthquakes in the eighties.

During a recent year, over the course of six months there was the Guatemala earthquake, which was North America's greatest killer disaster ever—22,000 lives were lost and a million left homeless. It caused untold grief, starvation, and disease in the 2,700 square miles of the quake zone. Three months later, a quake killing a thousand people rocked northern Italy, Yugoslavia, Austria, West Germany, Czechoslovakia, and Belgium; another, eight times as powerful, struck in southern Russia; within a few days a comparable one hit China, near the Burmese border. (Neither Russia nor China disclosed the number of casualties.) Next to be hit by an earthquake was the Vancouver area (the most severe earthquake there in fifty-four years), to be followed in a few days by a coast-to-coast rocker across Mexico. Within days, Peru was in the throes of another series of earthquake convulsions, a grim reminder of the 66,794 who had lost their lives in 1970 in what has been called the largest natural disaster in the history of the modern Americas. Then in short order Indonesia was victimized by an earthquake that killed an estimated 9,000 people, followed by one in the Philippines, where some 8,000 lost their lives.

And of course it was during that six month period that perhaps the worst killer earthquake in history struck, in the Greater Peking area, with the population of Tangshan being decimated. A report in the *Ming Pao* newspaper reckoned 900,000 dead, the *Hong Kong View*, with full reports in, estimated the dead at a million. The *View* pointed out that the Chinese word for earthquake is *tien-fan-ti-fu*, meaning "heaven tumbles, earth cracks," and warned that such a strong earthquake meant the fall of a dynasty. In four weeks Mao Tse-tung was dead. The Chinese tradition that God in heaven always has the last word was not dead.

Apart from Jesus Christ, who is alive forevermore, Mao Tse-tung, while he lived, was worshiped by more people than any other person ever. He called himself creator, redeemer, savior. A billion living and dead Chinese called him messiah, lord, everlasting sun. "My glory will I not give to another," warned God; "I the Lord of Hosts will come with . . . earthquake" (Isa. 42:8; 29:6). In the Book of Revelation we read of judgmental earthquakes yet to come. For example, in Revelation 11:13 we read that "at that very hour there was a severe earthquake and a tenth of the city collapsed" (NIV).

Earthquakes are on the increase everywhere. It is an inexorable law of nature. Seismologist Gabriel Lablanc declared that "once there has been an earthquake in an area, we know it will experience more earthquakes, and they will be of equal or greater magnitude." A case in point is Colorado, where until 1962 there was not a solitary measurable earthquake, according to the *New York Times*. Since then, over three thousand earthquakes have been registered.

As accurate a history of earthquakes as seismologists are able to assemble indicates that there were 137 "major" earthquakes in the fourteenth century; 174 in the fifteenth; 253 in the sixteenth, and so on up through this century, in which already we've had 2,250 "major" earthquakes. This works out in terms of major earthquakes to an increase of 2,189 percent in six centuries. "Forecast: EARTHQUAKE," the title of a *Time* cover story, gives a comprehensive account of how geophysicists from around the world are currently warning that in any of an astonishingly high number of increasingly heavily populated areas, a million or more people could, virtually without warning, be wiped out in a cataclysmic earthquake.

So then, both from the predictions of scientists and from the prophecies of the Bible, the future, insofar as earthquake destruction is concerned, looks bleak. Perhaps the most quoted seismologist in the world today is Dr. Don Anderson, director of the Caltech Seismology Laboratory, Pasadena. To the American Association for the Advancement of Science, Dr. Anderson warns of concrete "evidence the earth may soon suffer a number of cataclysmic earthquakes." He points out that "major earthquakes occur when the earth's daily rotation slows and when the North Pole wobbles away from its normal position with respect to the heavens." Anderson goes on, "The earth's rotation has been slowing at about one one-thousandth of a second daily for five years. And the North Pole has been wobbling as much as fifteen feet out of normal position." The conditions are ripening for "major disastrous earthquakes"—worldwide. When you add to this the fact that when the thirty-nation Disarmament Conference met in Geneva it was affirmed that it is now "conceivable in certain areas to provoke an earthquake or gigantic tidal wave," you reach the realization that the times are ripe for earthquakes to inflict destruction such as the world has never seen.

Some of the factors causing earthquakes are being probed today. In the past decade, the development of a bold new geological theory called "plate tectonics"—which offers an elegant, comprehensive explanation for continental drift, mountain building, and volcanism—seems finally to have clarified the underlying cause of earthquakes. It holds that the surface of the earth consists of about a dozen giant, 70-mile-thick rock plates. Floating on the earth's semimolten mantle and propelled by as-yet-undetermined forces, the plates are in constant motion. Where they meet, friction sometimes temporarily locks them in place, causing stresses to build up near the edges. Eventually the rock fractures, allowing the plates to resume their motion. It is said that sudden release of pent-up energy causes earthquakes.

As we turn to the Revelation and read what is ahead, let us keep in mind that the Middle East generally is one of the most earthquake-prone areas of the world. The recent earthquake in Turkey that killed three thousand took place where the seven churches of the Revelation had been located. Let us also keep in mind that Jesus said the Middle East is going to be the stage of the "great tribulation such as was not since the beginning of the world to this time, no, nor ever shall be" (Matt. 24:21 KJV). It will be a time when people will "flee to the mountains" (v. 16). When an earthquake hits, people inevitably do two things: they run for cover and they call out to God—in curses or in prayer. In a Palm Springs (California) high school hangs a sign which reads: "In the event of an earthquake, the Supreme Court ruling against prayers in school will be temporarily suspended."

Already people are sensing the omens. *Time* features an account of a sizable number of Californians who, for a fee of $12,500 joined the Doomsday Club, which endeavors to provide survival facilities in the Scott Meadows in the Sierras north of San Francisco for those who would otherwise perish in the expected apocalypse. Earlier in the 1970s *Time-Life* sponsored a documentary produced by the British Broadcasting Corporation entitled "The City That Waits to Die." As one of the sponsors explained, "We keep piling up people on the most dangerous fault on the planet"—San Francisco—where, as the fictionalized edition goes, 100,000 people are killed in the Bay area in the expected quake. Prior to this, of course, top pop songs featured such an earthquake, and a best seller was published, *The Late Great State of California*, the title from which Hal Lindsey derived his remarkable bestseller, *The Late Great Planet Earth*.

Ed McMahon, co-host on Johnny Carson's "Tonight Show," assures whoever will listen that experiencing an earthquake "in fact" differs sharply from experiencing one in pretense as in *Earthquake* or "The City That Waits to Die." "Anyone around Los Angeles that day will never forget February 9, 1971," noted McMahon. "I was hitting the sack about 4:00 A.M. An hour and fifty-nine minutes later, all hell broke loose. My first reaction was that some unseen force was trying to break down the walls of my room. . . . I was on the seventeenth floor and was positive our building was going to pitch too far and crash to the ground. I have had a couple of close calls flying in two wars, but I have never been more frightened than that morning. How do I feel about living on a shelf that is moving in the opposite direction from the shelf beneath it? When those two shelves grinding against each other have had it, maybe so have I," McMahon reflects. In fact, Mr. McMahon, the whole of mankind should be reminded, every time they read of, let alone experience, "earthquakes" that Jesus Christ is coming again and the end of the age is approaching. An earthquake is one of His means to call us to repentance as it was with the Philippian jailer (Acts 16:16-40).

The consummation of the age and the descent of the Son of God with His saints to reign throughout the world, bringing harmony out of chaos and beauty out of ashes, is recorded both in Revelation and Zechariah. In other words, disaster will precede the coming of Christ. Certain seismologists are warning of such a disaster in the Middle East, with Africa and Europe pushing at each other from beneath and Europe being shoved eastward and the Middle East westward. In Revelation 16:18-21 we read, "Then there came flashes of lightning, rumblings, peals of thunder and a severe earthquake. No earthquake like it has ever occurred since man has been on earth, so tremendous was the quake the great city split into three parts, and the cities of the nations collapsed. . . . Every island fled away and the mountains could not be found. From the sky huge hailstones of about a hundred pounds each fell upon men. And they cursed God on account of the plague of hail, because the plague was so terrible." It could be conjectured that God will simply allow natural laws in His universe to cause the polar ices to break up and storm over the continents in a cataclysmic blizzard, or it could be a shooting of water, say, eight or nine miles into the air where the temperature is minus forty degrees and the water freezes into ice balls. Who knows what God has in mind? A spectacular Alaskan volcanic eruption is but another reminder that in the world of nature over which God presides both beauty and terror await release!

In any event, in Zechariah 14:1-8 (NEB) we read: "Watch, for the day of the Lord is coming soon! On that day, the Lord will gather together the nations to fight Jerusalem; the city will be taken, the houses rifled, the loot divided, the women raped; half the population will be taken away as slaves, and half will be left in what remains of the city. The the Lord will go out fully armed for war, to fight against those nations. That day His feet will stand upon the Mount of Olives, to the east of Jerusalem, and the Mount of Olives will split apart, making a very wide valley running from east to west, for half the mountain will move toward the north and half toward the south. You will escape through that valley, for it will reach across to the city gate. Yes, you will escape as your people did long centuries ago from the earthquake in the days of Uzziah, King of Judah, and the Lord God shall come, and all the saints and angels with Him . . . there will be continuous day! Only the Lord knows how! There will be no normal day and night—at evening time it will still be light. Life-giving waters will flow . . . and the Lord shall be King over all the earth. In that day there shall be one Lord—His name alone will be worshipped."

What an event! Out of cataclysm and chaos a re-creation of resources will occur. It will be the solution to the energy crisis: "There will be continuous day!" and "life-giving waters will flow." Ralph Nader is currently on a crusade for the United States to turn from petroleum and nuclear power stations to a far more widespread use of the power of the sun, the wind, and water. When the Lord comes to set up His kingdom on earth, "at evening time it will still be light. Life-giving waters will flow" and when "the Lord shall be King over all the earth," the energy commission for the world will be in the hands of one Administrator: Jesus Christ!

The current energy and basic-materials crisis, which geophysicists face the world over, is one of man's greatest problems today. Professor Dennis Meadows, in his book *The Limits of Growth*, commissioned by the "Club of Rome," warns that the present rape of the earth's crust in search of energy sources is going to be man's ultimate undoing, if other destructive holocausts do not intervene. Meadows says, "When we realize that over the next fifteen years, we must mobilize as many raw materials as have been extracted during all of man's history on this globe [and that] over the next ten or fifteen years we must produce and install and bring into full operation as much power production capacity as has been accumulated up to this point in history, we begin to have some feeling for the rapid rate of change" and, we may add, the ultimate energy disaster that we are bringing down on our heads.

Much scientific conjecture has been advanced concerning the exhausting of our planet's resources and cracking the earth's crust through deep explosives and dislocations of vast oil reserves. It is not known what chain reaction effects there may be between humanly triggered detonations and eventual convulsions in nature.

As the late Bishop Fulton Sheen pointed out, the energy crisis is not only one of shortage but of distribution, noting that the population of the United States is six percent of the world's total and consumes one-third of the world's resources. For example, the United States burns up 20 million barrels of oil per day. American energy consumption over the last thirty years has more than doubled: from 37,000 trillion BTUs in 1950 to 80,000 trillion BTUs in 1980. Joseph H. Wherry, United States delegate to the United Nations International Symposium on Geothermal Energy in San Francisco, states that it is projected that United States energy needs by 1985 will go up from a current 460 million kilowatts to 700 million.

This consumption is perhaps not wrong—except in a relative sense: while we in the United States and Canada have so much, most of the world has so little. And what is worse, with warclouds lowering over the human race and there being no current answer to the shortages that are inevitably ahead of us, how much longer can we keep spending an annual of 600 billion dollars throughout the world on war weaponry? A great deal of this spending consumes energy that, if it were used to raise the standard of living for the underprivileged, underhoused, and underfed majority of earthlings, would greatly alleviate their plight.

Will our energy requirements come eventually from the sun, the center of the solar system? No! They will come from the Son of God whose access to energy reserves are more vast than the wealth of His mighty universe. His distribution will be as magnanimous as His reserves are enormous. "He is the image of the invisible God, the firstborn over all creation. For by Him all things were created: things in heaven and on earth, visible and invisible, whether thrones or powers or rulers or authorities; all things were created by Him and for Him. He is before all things, and in Him all things hold together" (Col. 15-17).

6

THE ECOLOGICAL SIGNS

Most of us, until the beginning of the seventies, had never consciously heard the word *ecology*. Then suddenly when we did, it seemed that we saw or heard it every time we picked up a newspaper or turned on our radio or television. It was on billboards, on school curricula from kindergarten to Ph.D. studies, and on the agenda of meetings of all kinds. Everything, it seemed, was involved in "the ecology crisis," until about 1973, when the energy crisis took over center stage. We learned that ecology was the branch of biology that deals with the relation of living things to their environment and to each other. We also learned that lawmakers—right from the parental level to the school, the municipal, the national, and the United Nations levels—were spending a great deal of time studying data and passing laws, because, they said, if the bombs didn't destroy us, an ecological disaster would. MIT scientists fed all the relevant data into the world's most sophisticated computer and came to the conclusion that man had about a generation to repent of his ecological crimes or he would perish from the earth. The Club of Rome concurred, and its solemn pronouncements were trumpeted around the world.

Within three years, the ecology kick got forced from the front pages to give way to other swords of Damocles, but we all knew from the facts that the pronouncements of its experts still stood. And as we head into the eighties, Maurice Strong, executive director of the Nairobi-based United Nations Environment Program (dubbed "The chief 'physician' of the world") warns us that ecologically, "this generation will determine the future of the human race . . . mankind must face the fact that doomsday is possible—even probable —if it continues on its present course." E. W. Scott, moderator of the World Council of Churches, fears that our current passion to solve the energy crisis may very well lead us to overlook the "ecology" catastrophe humanity faces. He laments that man is being "steamrollered into a destructive course of action" by adopting policies that will pollute to the point of poisoning his environment.

When Jesus' disciples asked Him what evidence signaling His second coming they should look for, He said that environmentally there will be, for starters, "pestilences" as "the beginning of sorrows." As they run their gamut, they will be a part of the "great tribulation, such as was not since the beginning of the world to this time, no, nor ever shall be" (Matt. 24:7,8,21 TEV). If those times of "plagues everywhere" (Luke 21:11 TEV) are to be unprecedented, they must exceed in decimation such plagues as, say, the Black Death of A.D. 1347, which allegedly wiped out a third of the world's known population. They must also exceed the Spanish influenza of 1918, which wiped out 20 million people, including 548,000 Americans. These precedents caused the U.S. Congress to pass a law to provide free for all Americans immunization shots against the swine-flu virus. In Revelation 6:7 we read of a quarter of the population of the earth being destroyed by war, famine, and "plague" in one great apocalyptic stroke.

Then there is the current worldwide pandemic of venereal diseases. We are informed that in Africa, currently, as many as 40 percent of the child-bearing women have V.D. In Sweden, sometimes called the "first of the enlightened countries" where "the new morality" has been pioneered, V.D. has shot up 750 percent over the last twelve years. Ottawa reports a 30 percent increase in V.D. in one year. In the United States in a year, gonorrhea has increased 21 percent. Of the 2.5 million Americans who currently have gonorrhea, it is estimated that 800,000 of these are women who do not yet know they have it. Meanwhile, they are passing it on to their sex partners. Angier Biddle Duke found out how serious gonorrhea is, when, for passing it on to Washington socialite Margaret Housen, a Wyoming Court ordered him to pay her $1,300,000 compensation.

The National Center for Disease Control of the United States has apprised the public through 1980 articles in such magazines as *Time* of the rising incidence of "herpes simplex two." Dr. Marion Powell warns: "Herpes has become an epidemic in North America. It is estimated that 50 million people have had herpes infection." Ann Landers apprises her 82 million daily readers: "We now have a form of V.D.—herpes simplex II—for which there is no cure."

Chatelaine magazine tells us that in Canada V.D. has doubled during the last decade and that most of the new cases strike those between the ages of fifteen and twenty-four. In fact, V.D. has already become a plague. Imagine what will happen during what Jesus called the "Great Tribulation," when there will be acute shortages of medicines and death will be all around, the normal restraints in society will all be disrupted, people will be in distress such as man has never known before, and the church of Jesus Christ will be gone. Promiscuous sex will undoubtedly be engaged in, with scarcely any inhibitions whatsoever, and the inevitable result will be a pandemic of V.D. gone wild.

What about antibiotics? Can they and other drugs control disease? Canada's most visible and quoted geneticist, Professor David Suzuki, warns that antibiotics cure the symptoms of a disease, not the disease itself. He goes on to say that "within the next few years North America will be defenseless against an epidemic because of its overdependence on antibiotics and other drugs . . . antibiotics are being pushed by pharmaceutical companies to such an extent that people across the continent are becoming resistant to them, leaving society defenseless against disease."

Chapter 7 deals with famine. But it is relevant here to point to a team of physicians who reckon, according to the *Philippines Times Journal* that already 800 million children growing up in the Third World are afflicted by disabling diseases, due, among other dire deficiencies, to protein malnutrition. According to the World Health Organization, there are in the world today approximately 60 million children with onchocerciasis, 210 million with filiariasis, and 220 million with schistosomiasis. *Time* tells us of a new worldwide epidemic of malaria "with a vengeance." In 1965, there were only 125,000 cases of malaria in India; now there are four million. In Pakistan, in 1961, there were 9,500 cases; now there are 10 million.

One of the problems, of course, is the way people are being jammed into cities, where pollution in terms of disease and atmospheric contamination leads experts like Vera Boikoff to conclude that "the world faces an ecological holocaust of a magnitude" unknown in human history.

Plato laid down the ideal size for a community of citizens as 5,040—the number who could gather in the Athenian marketplace. In the past fifteen years some 577 million have moved into communal aggregations of 100,000 or more people; projections tell us 1.4 billion will move in within the next twenty years. Under United Nations demographic definitions, "big cities" start at a half million. Then there are "million cities"; "multi-million cities" (over 2.5 million); and "superconurbations," like Tokyo, Yokohama, and greater New York, ranging from 12.5 million upward. By 1985, we're told, there will be three or four metropolitan areas with 25 million, two or three with 50 million, and by the end of the century, mathematical extrapolation tells us there will be 100-million cities if the present trend continues. This is in contrast to the fact that in the whole world, in 1950, there were only 75 cities with a million or more. It comes as a surprise to most people that already we have the following populations of cities, not counting their suburbs: Shanghai, 10,820,000; Tokyo, 8,841,000; New York, 7,895,000; Peking, 7,570,000; London, 7,379,000; Moscow, 7,050,000; Bombay, 5,969,000; Seoul, 5,536,000; Sao Paulo, 5,187,000; and Cairo, 4,961,000. Already the breakdown in public services (if they were ever installed), the inner-city decay, and the cultural deprivation of sprawling squalid slums are among the human ecological nightmares of our times.

This leads us to the ugly theme of air pollution. The *Wall Street Journal* laments that the zeal to cleanse the smog out of the big cities is now almost dead: "Back in 1970 everybody seemed to want clean air. President Nixon wanted it. Congress wanted it. Even college students were for it. So Congress decreed: Let there be clean air by 1975. . . . Congress created the Environmental Protection Agency to work out the details. By 1973, the E.P.A. had prescribed stiff cures for polluted, unhealthy air in 39 major cities." The *Journal* grieves, the hazards are as bleak as ever, but the people don't want to be bothered with remedies. So currently, Washington, D. C., where laws are made, has the highest air-pollution count ever, and one of the highest of any city in the world.

Currently we are seeing a movie *Blood on the Sun*. Jesus said that one of the events of that time of "Great Tribulation" will be that "immediately after the distress of those days, the sun will be darkened, and the moon will not give its light" (Matt. 24:29). Even in the ancient prophecy of Joel (2:30,31, KJV), the passage from which Peter quoted on the day of Pentecost, we read that on "the earth" there will be "pillars of smoke. The sun shall be turned into darkness, and the moon into blood, before the great and the terrible day of the Lord come." This same prophecy appears in Revelation 9:2, where we read that when "he opened the Abyss, smoke rose from it like the smoke from a gigantic furnace. The sun and the sky were darkened by the smoke from the Abyss." Revelation 6:12 states that "the sun turned black like sackcloth made of goat hair, the whole moon turned blood-red."

Of course, what we see now is only a portent of what is up ahead, but it certainly is indicative. Anyone who travels widely can recollect seeing the moon—or the sun—through the heavily polluted air of various cities, when the metallic content in the air pollution is heavy. The result is that the usually yellow rays that filter through are blood red. Frequently one can come from the beautiful sunshine of the countryside or above the clouds into one of the sprawling megalopolises of our times, and his sinuses tighten up, his nostrils burn, coughing is instinctive, and the sun is a globe veiled by soot, sort of like the flame of a lantern, back on the farm, when the glass shield was smoked up and needed badly to be cleaned.

And if just normal air pollution in the proliferating megalopolises of our times is bad, what will it be like if chemical warfare breaks out? The *U. S. News and World Report* tells us that "while the U.S. has officially renounced first-strike use of chemical weapons, the Soviet Union thinks differently, according to top NATO officials. During a recent Russian war game, NATO intelligence has learned, Soviet forces opened their simulated attack on Western Europe by blanketing Denmark with a gas that renders its victims unconscious for 48 hours." *Newsweek* reckons that according to United States intelligence Russian front-line rifle regiments in Central Europe are armed with poison gas artillery and mortar shells stored in the same bunkers as conventional weapons. Recently these bunkers were known to include germ-warfare weapons, and there is no current evidence that the Russians "are not constantly increasing these" bacteriological weapons. They used them in 1980 in their ruthless subjugation of Afghanistan.

A gas that is currently "hooking" and killing people prematurely throughout the world is tobacco smoke. Dr. William Foege, Director of the U.S. Center for Disease Control in Atlanta, asked the American Association for the Advancement of Science in 1981: "Is smoking the next third world woe?" He pointed out that "tobacco-related illness will be the Third World's major health problem within twenty years."

In the United States, the surgeon-general warns that in 1980, 85,000 Americans died from smoking. People who smoke two packs of cigarettes daily cut their life expectancy fourteen to fifteen years, women, nineteen to twenty years. When President Ford and Henry Kissinger were in China, the leaders there admitted that this was one habit the Chinese were not able to kick. Kissinger said it was the only bad habit his wife Nancy couldn't rid herself of, though she had gone to the best doctors for help. Asked how one can be healthy, the late Dr. Paul Dudley White counseled: first, "by eliminating tobacco."

Smoking is a virtually universal pollution of the air today—in China as in the United States, in Brazil as in the Soviet Union. In the United States annually 430 billion cigarettes are smoked. There are twice as many women classifying themselves as smokers as there were twenty years ago, and among teen-age girls, smoking has jumped an additional 5 percent during the 1970s—an odd way to celebrate women's liberation. Use of cigarettes by Americans averages 4,148 per year for each person over eighteen years of age. Despite banning cigarette ads on television and radio in most countries and the requirement to mark the packages with a warning that cigarettes are a health hazard, cigarette smoking is on the increase worldwide. For example, in Sweden, it has doubled in the last twenty years.

And in the proportion that smoking is increasing, so is cancer. In fourteen years, deaths from lung cancer among women has tripled. Deaths from cancer in the United States is steadily on the increase. Currently, it is responsible for one in four deaths in the United States. Two in every three families are victimized by cancer. It is no wonder that many call the cigarette "the cancer stick." Is it a part of what Jesus said would characterize the world before His coming again, namely, "epidemics"? (Luke 21:11 LB).

Throughout most of the world today, governments are

deliberately trying to discourage the pollution of our environment. But the coming Antichrist will be characterized by his deliberate provocation of "abomination that causes desolation" (Mark 13:14). While this has a specific application, it also is going to be a typical trait of his pernicious regime.

Jesus said that a part of the horrible scenario of the "Great Tribulation," along with the signs in the sun and moon above, will be that "on the earth nations will be in anguish and perplexity at the roaring and tossing of the sea" (Luke 21:25). Revelation 8:8,9 tells us that at that time the seas will be thrown into terrible convulsion, with the result that "a third of the living creatures in the sea" will die and then a vast, contaminating star "wormwood" will poison "a third of the rivers" and "springs of water" of the world, and "many people [will die] from the waters" (Rev. 8:8-10). The Roman Catholic Bishops of Canada lamented that in the 1980s, 8 million die annually from contaminated water. Then we turn to the warning of Brian Crozier, director of the institute for the Study of Conflict to the American Senate Judiciary Committee, that terrorist guerrillas are very seriously "exploring the possibility of poisoning the water supply of a major city."

And what is comparably disturbing, and attracting a great deal of attention in the 1980s, is the acid rain pollution of our inland waters. John Roberts, Canada's environment minister, complains that already "acid rain has denuded several hundred Canadian lakes of fish."

Sydney Harris points out that two-thirds of the world's population currently lives in coastal areas, on space that, altogether, amounts to only 12 percent of the world's land mass; and that in twenty-five years, this will be true in the United States. Were the polar ice cap melted, say, by vast thermonuclear explosions, the oceans and seas and river mouths of the world would rise in great tidal waves that would drown hundreds of millions of people outright and pollute the residences of hundreds of millions of others, so as to render them uninhabitable.

Jacques Cousteau, the famous French oceanographer, tells us that the world's oceans, especially around highly populated areas, are becoming irreversibly polluted: "In 1967, I would say that 25 percent of the oceans' vitality has been lost in the last twenty years. Now, I would say that 40 to 50 percent of that vitality has been lost. Fish are disappearing; plants are disappearing." Henry Kissinger warns that "mankind's growing dependence on the seas, and the burgeoning world population along their shores are already burdening the ecology of the oceans—a development of potentially catastrophic significance. A cooperative international regime to govern the use of the oceans and their resources is therefore an urgent necessity." A check on the ocean fishing industry of the world confirms this. From 1950 to 1970, the world fish catch climbed steadily from twenty to seventy million tons. Since then, the catch has declined in consecutive years, even though the amounts of capital and effort expended continue to rise. Marine biologists are universal in their appeal for the ecological reform of this undermining of the oceans.

Ancient prophecies, of course, were written in Israel, whose sea was the Mediterranean. The United Nations Environment Program is seriously wondering if the Mediterranean has not already gone past the point of no return in terms of pollution, as every day from its vast fleets of ships, choked harbors, and 150 ever-growing cities an uncalculated tonnage of slag, oily spill, untreated raw sewage, and industrial effluent are discharged into its waters. In innumerable areas, the fishing and tourist industries are being forced to the wall, while such diseases as typhoid, dysentery, viral hepatitis, and polio are all currently epidemic. The annual 10 million tourists are finding that to swim is to come out with a scum of oil over their bodies. They also run the risk of infection from sewage pollution. If they eat fish in seaside restaurants, there is the chance they will ingest unhealthy quantities of mercury and other toxic substances passed on in the food chain.

Dean Rusk, in a speech to four thousand educators,

wonders out loud if there will be any worthwhile life in the oceans in ten years to support green life, reasoning further that marine life produces the oxygen with which land life is sustained. Is man upsetting the balance of nature beyond repair? Armond Fruchart, another famous oceanographer, says, "Man in the year 2000 probably will not die of hunger but of suffocation, for lack of clean air, or of thirst, for lack of pure water."

We noticed that a part of the "Great Tribulation" on the earth would be "the roaring." The pollution of our sound waves, immediate and electronic, is another factor that bombards modern man. The Geneva International Standardization Organization warns that "if urban noise continues to grow at its present rate of one decibal per year, most city-dwellers will be stone deaf by the year 2000." When the United States congress was considering whether or not they would allow the British and French Concordes to land in American airports, they had to decide on the basis of the noise limit set by the Heathrow airport in London at 110 perceived noise decibels, whereas the Concorde cannot become airborne when loaded without emitting 134. And as to music: when I was a boy, popular music tended to be soft and sweet. Much of today's music is loud and vulgar, and as Sydney Harris points out, the perceived noise decibels at an ordinary rock concert are "four times greater than would be permitted in an industrial plant for fear of permanent damage to the eardrums of the auditors." *The Guinness Book of World Records* claims that the Rolling Stones have blasted out a world record, holding 120 decibels during a recent London concert. The loudest woman is Gracie Hall, 65 years old, who shouted a 108.6-decibel "roar" in a village in Devon, England.

Jesus assured us that the destructive forces in the "Great Tribulation" would come so near to doing in the whole surviving human race on earth that "except those days should be shortened, there should no flesh be saved: but for the elect's sake those days shall be shortened" (Matt. 24:21,22 KJV). It is now well known and proved that radioactive fallout from atomic energy and nuclear fission is devastating to human life—and all other life. Current newspapers are replete with articles on the fact that radioactive emissions from nuclear power stations have to be carefully contained and buried for 25,000 years before they lose their lethal effect. The Club of Rome warns that "a plutonium bell the size of a grapefruit contains enough poison to annihilate the population of the planet. Furthermore, plutonium's radioactivity lasts 25,000 years. And we would have to produce and transport 15 million kilos every year! Truly, betting on the atom is like signing a contract with the devil."

During a recent meeting between United States and Russian scientists on the theme of man's "fear of apocalyptic weather weapons, perhaps even worse than the fear of nuclear arms," it was stated that the scientists in both countries either have, or are on the edge of developing, means for making "man-made fog, rain, snow, hurricanes," and "tidal waves." In addition, he may be on the verge of wittingly or accidentally destroying "the ozone layer in the upper atmosphere to expose the population underneath to lethal doses of ultraviolet rays."

A very mysterious destruction is to be effected in the time of the Great Tribulation when, it is said in the language of prophecy, "locusts came from the smoke and descended on the earth" to "attack people" (Rev. 9:3). The *New York Times* carries an astonishing article on the threat of locusts on the peoples of the Middle East and Africa. It describes three occasions in the last ninety years when three different kinds of locusts threatened all life in the swath of their destruction. In one, "a swarm of locusts some 2,600 square miles in area, crossed the Red Sea in what amounted to re-enactment of one of the biblical plagues of Egypt." Another was during World War II when swarms affected considerably the outcome of military operations in North Africa. Another was in 1967, when swarms that evolved on both sides of the Red Sea flew clear across Africa to the Atlantic. The *Times* concludes that under certain circumstances "plagues" are brought about by locusts that because of peculiar "environmental conditions" were made "to proliferate" and through "radical change" go forth and work unpredictable and perhaps near-total destruction. *Time* runs a cover story entitled "The Bugs Are Coming," quoting from *The Hellstrom Chronicle*: "If any living species is to inherit the earth, it will not be man." The coming again of Jesus, of course, annuls this statement. But, suffice it to say, a reading of this article and then the Book of Revelation would lead one to believe that apart from Christ's return, insects would indeed take over the world.

The apostle Paul gives us a prophetic description of the days of the antichrist, noting that "the mystery of iniquity doth already work" (2 Thess. 2:7 KJV). One of the most mysterious phenomena to modern medical science is the way drugs affect the human anatomy. There is a mystery about drugs that has prevented the best minds from comprehending precisely what makes them react on the human anatomy as they do. But that their legal misuse and illegal abuse is one of the foremost pollutions of man in our time is beyond doubt.

Although drug abuse is not receiving the ubiquitous attention in the later seventies that it did in the earlier seventies, it has not receded in its assault on man. Elsewhere, we note the link that it has to Satanism as dealt with in the Book of Revelation, for at the time of World War III it will be the agency to release the demons, who in turn will incite the leaders of the world to gather in the Middle East for Armageddon. But here we must look at drug abuse as one of the foremost pollutants of our time. The *New York Times* recently published the findings of the United States government-sponsored National Institute on Drug Abuse. This institute disclosed that in the last two years marijuana use among fourteen- and fifteen-year-olds has more than doubled: from 10 percent to 22 percent. Half of the high school seniors have at least tried marijuana, while 56 percent of the eighteen- to twenty-year-olds currently smoke it on a regular basis. The institure "called the increased use of all types of drugs, especially among younger children, alarming." The Drug Abuse Council, after polling Americans, states that 29 million American adults have used marijuana. A son of a former United States president amazed millions when he rationalized his own experimentation with marijuana as being a part of the youth scene seeking meaning when there are "so many problems with the disillusionment and alienation of young people in this country."

Hard drugs present another problem. CBS News has run a special on "The Mexican Connection" of brown heroin, reckoning that more heroin enters the United States currently than ever before. The *New York Times* quotes narcotics officer Sterling Johnson, as speaking for New York City, and federal drug-enforcement official Michael Costello, as speaking for the nation as a whole, that in about 1973, it looked like the hard-drugs craze had peaked. It had, and it leveled off. Then suddenly it began its ugly climb again, with the increase now topping by far all previous highs. In 1980, deaths from heroin in New York shot up 46 percent, according to the *New York Times*.

With the ecological atmosphere of our planet becoming more and more darkened, portending World War III, only Christ's coming again will provide "Son Light" enough to break through the cloud of man-made pollution.

7

THE BIOLOGICAL SIGNS

When the disciples asked Jesus what would be the sign of (or the scenario at) the time of His coming again and the end of the age, He replied that insofar as people's intake of food and drink was concerned, "there will be famines . . . in different parts of the world" (Matt. 24:7, PHILLIPS). In Revelation 6:5, 6 (a passage used by a *Toronto Star* editorial to caption the current tragic spread of famine over the earth) we see this same projected scene: "When the lamb opened the third seal, I heard the third living creature say, 'Come!' I looked, and there before me was a black horse! Its rider was holding a pair of scales in his hand. Then I heard what sounded like a voice among the four living creatures saying, 'A quart of wheat for a day's wages, and do not damage the oil and the wine!'"

The black horse is symbolic of famine. In other Scriptures, such as Jeremiah 4:28 or Lamentations 4:8, 9, black is associated with famine spreading over the land. In Revelation 6:8 we read that a killer famine will spread "over a fourth of the earth." So that in the future we can expect famine to spread in various places throughout the world. The black horse carries a rider who has a pair of scales in his hands—a symbol that apparently indicates careful rationing. It would take meticulous rationing indeed to distribute an income of a quart of wheat for a day's work! Certainly the breadwinner in any household would have all he or she could do to earn enough to feed one person, let alone a family. So the poverty in some parts of the world will verge on famine and in many places will lead to stark, mass starvation.

Signs of the black horse of Revelation 6, of Jesus' warning that there will be famines in different parts of the world, are ubiquitous today. No one who believes in the return of Christ can see, firsthand, the countless pitifully starving people in the world today without sighing, "Even so, come, Lord Jesus!" (Rev. 22:20 KJV).

Biologists Paul Erlich of Stanford University, William and Paul Paddock, and the late Sir Julian Huxley give great sections of the human race virtually no hope of avoiding proliferating famine. Commenting gravely on the years immediately ahead, Erlich notes, "There is not the slightest hope of escaping a disastrous time of famines," for from this moment onward "it is shockingly apparent that the battle to feed man will end in a rout." The Paddocks reckon that from here on in, "famines, greater than any in history, will ravage the underdeveloped nations!" The CBS Evening News reckons currently, an annual 60 million humans starved to death in famines around the world—six times as many as those who starved to death in 1970. The World Food Conference in Rome estimates the current annual famine toll at 62 million. This amounts to 170,000 people every day of the year. That's like all the people of Madison starving to death in a twenty-four-hour period, or all the people of Seattle in a week, or all the people of Philadelphia in a month, or all the people of the British Isles in a year—wiped out in an all-voracious famine. *Time* reckons a half billion humans are "starving" slowly.

Leighton Ford says on the worldwide "Hour of Decision": "A decade ago we heard dire warnings that famine would grip vast portions of planet earth by the 1970s. Then it seemed incredible; today . . . the famine is here. . . . Nearly half a billion people are suffering from some form of hunger, living on what Mahatma Gandhi called 'an eternal compulsory fast.' Children in the refugee camps of Bangladesh are so emaciated they look deformed."

The World Council of Churches, in their concluding statement of the Nairobi Council lamented, "The world is on a catastrophic course leading to mass starvation." *Time's* Nairobi Bureau Chief, Lee Griggs, spent eighteen months on a "terribly depressing" assignment: looking at famine over a fifteen-thousand-mile trek. He said that "watching people die slowly from starvation is worse than watching them die quickly in war. The look of utter despair on their faces is something I'll never forget. . . . It's the children and babies your heart goes out to most, and to mothers who stare vacantly at you as they try to suckle babes at dried-up breasts."

Bob Hope came back from one of his safaris into areas of starvation to remonstrate, "The scraps we toss in the garbage would be a sumptuous meal for them." Commenting on hunger in India, *Time* estimates that only half of India's 600 millions eat more than one meal a day. Tom Harpur writes from Africa that you have to see it to believe it—some of the conditions in which people in underdeveloped countries live. Eight hundred million of them, in addition to hunger, have to cope with "living in squalid, dehumanizing shacks and camps." A United Nations report goes so far as to state that in the long history of man "it is doubtful whether such a critical food situation has ever been so worldwide." We are grappling," says India'a health and family-planning minister, "with the most serious problem any nation has ever had to deal with"—impending starvation.

Girdling the globe at its equatorial bulge is a belt of hunger. Above it live the 1.4 billion inhabitants of the northern developed nations whose advanced industry and agriculture permit them the luxury of worrying about reducing diets instead of diet deficiencies. Below it are the potentially prosperous lands of the southern hemisphere's temperate zone. The only exportable food surpluses now left in the world are produced by the highly capitalized agricultures of the larger industrialized countries, including Australia, Argentina, Canada, and the United States, which have in recent years produced twice their own domestic food requirements. Europe and China produce about as much food as they consume. While Americans are a billion pounds overweight, and Canadians a hundred million pounds, and both are for the most part trying to cut down on eating, much of the world is trying to find something to eat.

Most of the 2.5 billion citizens of the underdeveloped world live in the equatorial belt. *Time* states that nearly all of them are ill-fed, at least 60 percent are malnourished, and 20 percent more are starving. Today, famine is rampant in Bangladesh, Ethiopia, the African nations of the Sahel (Chad, Mali, Mauritania, Niger, Senegal, and Upper Volta), Gambia, and areas of Tanzania and Kenya. Near-famine also plagues Bolivia, Syria, Yemen, and parts of northern Nigeria. One poor harvest could bring massive hunger to India, the Sudan, Guyana, Somalia, Guinea, and Zaire. Of course, Angola, with its wars, verges on starvation. In a score of other countries the populace faces chronic food shortages, among them are Indonesia, the Philippines, and Haiti.

The Soviet Union does not at this time face mass famine. But as it enters the eighties, it does so with a more critical food situation than it has faced previously in this half of the century. Its projected grain crop expectations of 215.7 million tons for a year recently turned out to be a 137-million-ton crop—78.7 million tons short of its needs. *U.S. News and World Report* notes that "for the first time in years, ordinary Russians are talking about possible food shortages. . . . This year's disastrous grain harvest is reducing bread supplies," and "there are reports of rationing."

Russia does, however, have sufficient influence and affluence to buy its basic food requirements. But this has the effect of reducing the total world food reserves to the point that, according to the private reckoning of a former United States cabinet member, the earth's food reserves are down now to a precarious 13½ days of consumption. One Washington official said that in contrast to the surpluses of the late 1960s, when it was nearly inconceivable that the tables could be so bare, man is now witnessing "the virtual disappearance of the world's surplus food stocks." The president of the American Can Company said to Billy Graham, "Right in this country, we're one crop away from a famine." It must be kept in mind that the responsibility for food production rests on precariously few Americans today. When the Declaration of Independence was signed two hundred years ago, 95 percent of the American people grew food. Now the farming population is down to 5 percent.

Several critical areas of possible solution need to be looked at. There is, of course, the matter of overpopulation. Kurt Waldheim, Secretary General of the United Nations, reckons man's greatest despair is "the unprecedented growth of the world's population." Approximately one-quarter of all the people who have ever lived are alive today. The human race numbered a half billion when Jesus was on earth, a billion a century ago, two billion in 1920, four and a half billion today, and at its present rate of increase will double to nine billion in a single generation. The McWhirter brothers of London, authors of *The Guinness Book of World Records*, have calculated that given the present geometric rate of human population increase, by A.D. 2500, there would be one person for every square yard on earth; by A.D. 3700, humanity would outweigh the earth itself; and by A.D. 7975, there would be enough bodies to fill all space in the known universe.

Returning from hypothesis to reality, what is so grave, according to United Nations projections, is that 85 percent of the increase of the world's population in the remainder of this century will be in the underdeveloped countries, where, on the average, populations will double in thirty years if they continue at their present 3-percent-per-year rate of increase. What is of grave concern is that the underdeveloped countries by their rampant population explosions are on a collision course with starvation.

Birth control—that's the answer, say many in the Western world. Not so, says Pope John Paul II and the official Catholic Church worldwide. Artificial birth control, warns the Pope, is fraught with "serious consequences," and he assures the world that the stand of the Catholic Church will not change. As 130 countries send delegates to the United Nations World Population Conference in Bucharest, Rumania, the American delegation warns that failure to universalize artificial birth control will imperil the world in the 1980s. The Soviet Union and China, countered that the West's concern to impose artificial birth control was part of an "imperialist" myth aimed at keeping the developing countries in subjugation. The underdeveloped nations generally have resisted birth control as not being the answer: They insist instead that "industrial nations should share their wealth with poor countries in a new economic framework." This was a rather blunt reply to such committed advocates of artificial birth control as Senior Editor Marshall Loeb of *Time*, who editorializes that a look at the jarring mathematics of starvation reveals "the crisis will get worse until we in the West demand that the underdeveloped countries decrease their population growth."

But will these demands be effective? Objectively, after years of trying to sell birth-control promotions to the underdeveloped countries, Dr. Justin Blackwelder of the Environmental Fund in Washington, D. C., concedes, "Birth control simply isn't working. Couples in most impoverished countries want a large number of children because many will die. Children, you see, are the parents' only security in their old age." And so the populations of the underdeveloped countries are soaring upward in a hopeless spiral. And in African nations, according to *Time*, since the early 1960s, the per capita consumption of food has fallen 5 percent.

And what has the skyrocketing price increases of the last few years done to the food production potential of the underdeveloped countries? The *South China Morning Post* carries an article on "Food, Fuel, and Fertilizer," in which a Chinese writer argues very closely and rationally that the trebling of wheat prices was not nearly as serious a blow to the underdeveloped countries as the quadrupling of oil prices, on which agricultural equipment runs. Most serious of all, insofar as food production was concerned, was the trebling of the price of commercial fertilizers, an increase that occurred because 93 percent of the fertilizers of the world are petro-chemically based. The *Times Journal* in Manila notes that countries like India would have to spend four-fifths of their export earnings if they were to fill their oil needs. This cuts drastically into the fertilizer budget, and the result has been a tragic worsening of the food situation.

And as if this isn't enough, it appears that there may be a calamitous turn for the worse in the world weather patterns of the future, insofar as food production is concerned. The Russians certainly are currently wondering after "a summer drought hit the European U.S.S.R. In October rains, frost, and snow blighted Central Asian grain fields. Prematurely freezing temperatures killed winter wheat in the Ukraine" *(Time)*.

The CIA has astonished most of us by warning that a temperature drop of only one degree—*one degree!*—in the northern hemisphere would mean that India would have a major drought every four years, and China a major famine every five years; Canada's food production would be reduced by 50 percent.

Fortune published a carefully documented article entitled: "Ominous Changes in the World's Weather" in which it is stated that "in the first half of this century, the world enjoyed better weather than appears to have prevailed in at least a thousand years. During that period the world's population doubled. But now, say climatologists, the climate is rapidly returning to a less kindly norm. If this trend continues, says University of Wisconsin climatologist Reid Bryson, it will affect the whole human occupation of the earth—like a billion people starving. The change is not only the worldwide cooling that began in the forties, but an alteration of the planet's atmospheric circulation that comes about because of that cooling." *Fortune* demonstrates how floods, droughts, and other seemingly freakish weather shifts are the inevitable and ever-accentuating result. *Time* in various articles, shows how, since 1968, the Sahara desert has expanded 100 miles southward in some places; and how the arctic ice composite has expanded very substantially (an exact map is given), in some places 150 miles, and in most places about 50 miles.

Dr. Hurd C. Willard and a team of scientists at the Massachusetts Institute of Technology explains that planet Earth is gradually headed toward another irreversible ice age, which will progressively make itself evident over the next 125 years.

Dr. Reid Bryson (of the University of Wisconsin), taking direct aim at solving the food problem for the "ninety million" who are being added to the human family annually, came up abjectly pessimistic. Pointing to the Arctic ice accumulation insofar as it affects climate, he predicts "this Arctic cooling has a devastating effect on the tropical and subtropical areas. That's where most of the world's people live." Polar ice, stresses Bryson, spells the proliferation of human starvation. Dealing with this same grave theme, a body of American, Mexican, and Canadian climatologists meet in Toronto as guests of the Science Council of Canada. They warn world governments of their catastrophic "myopia" in failing to act on the fact that "greater swings in the climate—extremes of warm and cold, wet and dry—are going to occur over the next few decades and the people responsible for social and economic planning had better start taking this fact into account."

An example of these climate shifts came in early 1981, when Florida had its coldest January on record, the frost wiping out one-fourth of its orange crop and one-third of its vegetables. On January 15, it was warmer in the Canadian Yukon than it was in Florida.

Just what relationship does this grave biological prospect of proliferating human famine have on the matter of World War III and the coming again of Jesus Christ? Dean Rusk, in the 1970s, told a gathering of four thousand educators that the matter of starvation was one, which, if not solved, would bring on a war out of sheer human desperation. Man can expect "wars as nations struggle for territory to accommodate population pressures," editorializes the *Philadelphia Inquirer*. According to *Time*, key leaders today have many "fears that radical poor nations" will coerce more productive nations into "giving up their wealth by threatening a nuclear holocaust." Tanzania's Julius Nyerere, speaking for the "Group of 77, a consortium of developing countries [actually, there are now 103] within the United Nations," said to the Commonwealth Society in London recently, "It is not right that the vast majority of the world's people should be forced into the position of beggars without dignity. We demand change, and the only question is whether it comes by dialogue or confrontation." Is this one more milestone along the road to World War III?

Finally, let it be said that there is One who is concerned about housing and feeding the world. It is Jesus! *Time* asks if there is really anyone who cares that a third of mankind lives in near hopeless despair. There they are, in every quadrant of the world, "whether they are called *favelas, ranchos, bustees, barriadas,* or *bidonuilles,* there is a tragic sameness about these hovels where millions live and die: the fragile shacks made of cardboard or rusting corrugated sheet metal, the famished children's distended bellies, the inescapable stench of human beings packed tightly together without ready access to water or toilets." Will Jesus allow the social situation of the world to deteriorate much longer? Because He is God, and God is good, He's got to come back soon!

Meanwhile, Christians are to be in the vanguard of social compassion. Read again Jesus' Sermon on the Mount. Read again of His pronouncements at the judgment as recorded in Matthew 25. Read again about Christ's feeding the five thousand—and the four thousand. May we,

His disciples, keep telling that story. And let us not forget that all four evangelists recorded the feeding of the five thousand, the only miracle recorded in all four gospels. It is a part of the gospel of Jesus Christ. The ultimate gospel message, however, is that Jesus Christ is coming again to set up His kingdom of peace and plenty.

Meanwhile, as Billy Graham said to the 2,500 delegates to the Religious Broadcasters Convention in Washington in January 1981: "I do not believe in unilateral disarmament. But how can we be indifferent to the millions and millions who live on the brink of starvation each year, while the nations of the world spend $550 billion each year on weapons?"

8

THE ECONOMICAL SIGNS

Jesus did not say that a sign of His coming again and of the end of the age would be universal famine. Rather, He said that there would be "famines" in "different parts of the world" (Matt. 24:7, Phillips). Later in the same passage He indicated that in other parts of the world, whole peoples or blocs of nations would be "eating and drinking" as if there were no tomorrow. Indeed, they would adopt the stance that since "the Lord won't be coming for awhile," they might as well move into swingdom and live for "partying and getting drunk" (vv. 48,49, LB). In today's papers we're seeing accounts of social parties costing $100,000; of more and more homes in the multi-million dollar bracket; of pearl necklaces for Persian cats and of sumptuous poodle dog banquets.

The fact that before Christ returns, whole cultures will be caught up in a combination of an obsession with wealth, pleasure madness, and intemperance that will involve gluttony and drunkenness is seen in several passages. Paul wrote to Timothy, "You must face the fact: the final age of this world is to be a time" when people will "love nothing but money"; they will be intemperate; and they will "put pleasure in the place of God" (2 Tim. 3:1-4 NEB). It will be a time when there will be plenty of people with plenty of money—for a while—but with the apocalyptic events happening all around and the impending collapse of society nagging at them, they will worry about their insecurities and this will have a pressure-cooker effect on people. A Gallup polling of twenty-one nations in 1981 shows grave pessimism about the economic future. In his last appearance on television, the late Arnold Toynbee noted that already it's happening: "The expectation of people is that every year they will get richer and richer, and they're not going to. How will they take this?" For one thing, by a compulsive turning to "partying and getting drunk."

"Alcohol is a factor in 10 percent of all deaths in the United States, and one in 10 adult drinkers is likely to become an alcoholic," according to a U.S. congressional report in 1981. Alcoholic consumption increases about 3 percent per year and currently is a chief contributing factor to 75 percent of the divorces, 60 percent of the fatal automobile accidents, 50 percent of the homicides, and one-third of the suicides. The National Institute on Alcohol Abuse and Alcoholism reckons that alcoholism currently costs Americans 40 billion dollars per year, enough money to feed all the people around the world who are starving to death. What is perhaps most tragic is that the very young are drinking as they never have before. It is estimated that there are a half million alcoholics who are still children. The Research Triangle Institute study reckons that "28% of U.S. students in grades 7 through 12 are problem drinkers."

Dr. George Strachan, a Canadian whose seventeen-year-old son was killed while driving a car in a drunken stupor, avows that there are one million alcoholics untreated in Canada today. Since 1970, automobile fatalities caused by drivers eighteen to twenty-one years old who were under the influence of alcohol have soared by 350 percent in Ontario.

North America is not the world's chief offender in alcoholism. In France, over half of the patients in hospitals are there because of alcoholism. In Britain, "doctors have a very serious drinking problem": three and a half times the national average, notes Dr. Julius Merry, director of the alcoholic unit at West Park Hospital outside London. The *U.S. News and World Report* states that the Soviet Union has "a drunkenness problem that is one of the world's worst." Throughout the world, alcoholism as a killer is only behind heart disease and cancer.

When we turn again to the passage in Revelation 6:5,6, dealt with in the preceding chapter, and read of the black horse and its rider as a harbinger of proliferating famine, it is important to note that the rider on the black horse does not "damage the oil and the wine"—the fare of the rich. There will be people in whole sections of society who, while "Lazaruslike" sections are snatching at scraps, will "fare sumptuously every day." This can be seen in Revelation 18, where the Babylonian civilization revived (think of the Arab oil money turning poverty into paradises) will, right up to the era of Armageddon (WW III) indulge to the hilt their "wine, and oil, and fine flour, and wheat, and cattle, and sheep, and horses, and chariots." Anyone who has been around an Arab oil capital recently certainly has seen these luxury status symbols made possible by oil: the best in wines and liquors, steaks, the world's most beautiful horses and ostentatious chariots—cars, if you will—and the people certainly "clothed in fine linen, and purple, and scarlet, and decked with gold, and precious stones, and pearls." Yes, and the "so great riches . . . made rich all that had ships in the sea" (Rev. 18:13, 16, 17, 19 KJV). The huge oil tankers carrying oil from the Middle East are vehicles of riches such as the world has never yet known.

There is today a "Babylonian existence" (as Max Lerner described North American greed) apart altogether from a Babylonian revival. Harvard nutritionist Jean Mayer points out that if the grain that is used currently to make alcoholic beverages in North America alone were distributed evenly to the famine regions of the world, it would turn the starvation tide around. In fact, if the 16 million tons of grain currently going into making alcoholic beverages in North America alone were sent instead to the 60 million earthlings who, at a minimum, will starve to death this year, they would each have two and a half pounds of grain per day. That would be enough for them and more.

But this kind of sharing is not going to take place until Christ comes again. In fact, the conflict between the rich and poor nations is going to sharpen. "There is only one class," Oscar Wilde once noted, "that thinks more about money than the rich, and that is the poor. The poor can think of nothing else." And so the underdeveloped nations of the world get poorer and poorer. Two of the 4–5 billion peoples of the world have personal annual incomes of under $200. For example, a Pakistani's average per capita income is $130; an Indian's, $110; an Indonesian's, $80; and a Bangladeshan's, $70.

Contrast this with the average current per capita income of the following: the Arab emirates, $22,060; the Kuwaitan, $20,700; the Quataran, $10,530; the Swiss, $7,270; the Swede, $6,840; the Dane, $6,800; the American, $6,595; the Canadian, $6,340; the West German, $6,215; the Norwegian, $5,820; the Frenchman, $5,390; the Australian, $5,370; the Briton, $3,385. It should be pointed out that if the purchasing power of a nation's currency above taxes is used as a standard of measurement, then apart from the Arab oil nations, the United States still ranks first.

And whatever other impressions have been communicated, North Americans are going into the ninth decade of the twentieth century very much wealthier than they did into the sixth. It is true that in the last twenty-five years, prices in the United States have gone up 100 percent. But it is also true that paychecks have risen an average of 200 percent. Each American, on the average, is worth $26,530 today. In Canada, from 1950 to 1980, personal incomes have gone up 500 percent. The apostle James prophesied that near the close of this age many peoples will "have hoarded wealth." James further chides, "You have lived on earth in luxury and self-indulgence. You have fattened yourselves" (James 5:3,5).

Simultaneously with this terrific accumulation of wealth, North Americans have grown tired of giving handouts to the needy of the world. They see the ubiquitous invasion of eastern gurus like Hare Krishna and Maharaj Ji and realize how true Nehru's statement was, that it is simply unheard of that a Hindu religionist would inspire the building of a single dam or the plowing of a single field to alleviate poverty. North Americans are confused and angry that suddenly Arab capitalists have bounded by them in wealth, yet for their starving neighbors, as *Time* puts it, "conspicuously absent from the ranks of the generous are the newly rich Middle East oil exporters." The communists always give a shoestring with strings (of steel) attached—if they give at all. So it is hardly surprising that you can pick up magazines, newspapers, watch television, and discuss the matter with legislators and find that apart from those who give out of deep compassion, the reaction of the majority is everywhere something like this, as one person put it: "We've had a bellyful of doling out welfare to a thankless world. We've spent a generation past, sacrificing for a freeloading world, only to get kicked in the teeth." International charity sponsors are giving reporters stories that produce headlines like the one that appeared recently in The *Toronto Star*: "Canadian Public Is Unresponsive." British Prime Minister Margaret Thatcher announced she would scale down aid from 1.8 billion in 1980-1981 to 1.6 billion in 1982-83. The U.S. reduced overseas aid from .27 percent of its GNP in 1978 to .19 percent in 1979, and so on downward. The West generally and especially Americans are definitely tired of being the breadbasket, the wardrobe, the roofing agency, and the policemen of the world. And North Americans are not alone in this cynical hardening against the world's food plight. Three world conferences sponsored by the United Nations were held, respectively, in Bucharest on population control, in Rome on food, and in Vancouver on world housing ("habitat"). The impression left by all three was definitely that from here on in it would be humanity's inhumanity to man, and each for his own; not quite as bald as that, perhaps, but almost!

Meanwhile, as NBC notes in February 1981, 44 million North Americans spend 14 billion dollars annually on weight reduction: while a third of the world tries to get started eating, we're trying to stop. Jesus said that many at His coming would be preoccupied, not only with "drinking" but also with "eating," North Americans and Europeans consume half of the world's food and it is quality food, or at least expensive food. Senator Mark Hatfield points to the fact that Americans have increased their annual meat consumption between 1950 and 1975 from 55 pounds to 110 per capita. Leighton Ford told us on the "Hour of Decision" that it takes 20 pounds of grain to produce a pound of beef and that the same amount of food that feeds 210 million Americans would feed 1.5 billion Asians. How does that figure? *Christianity and Crisis* notes that only about 400 pounds of grain per year are available to the average person in less-developed countries—almost all consumed directly to meet minimal energy needs. By contrast, the average North American consumes 2,000 pounds, both directly (as bread, pastries, and breakfast cereals); and indirectly (in the form of meat, milk, and eggs). Therefore the average North American requires five times as many agricultural resources as the average Indian, Nigerian, or Colombian.

Biologist William Paddock points out that if America were to become completely vegetarian, its agriculture could support another 800 million people more than it does. CBS' "Dateline" claims that more than half of Iowa's corn goes to the birds in the fields and the cattle in the feed lots, and suggests—tongue in cheek—that farmers return to scarecrows and pastureland.

The average North American is frankly tired of having his conscience lashed with these facts. True, Mahatma Gandhi may have said, "The earth provides enough for everyman's need, but not for everyman's greed," but who wants to sit around and morbidly groan about the hungry of the world? We would prefer to stroke our 81 million household dogs and cats, which eat not only the quantity of food on which 53 million hungry people of, say, Africa, could fare very well. The pope may have ushered in a new year with an exhortation to the West to make this a year of feeding the famished of the world; the Archbishop of Canterbury, may tell us in Toronto that what we throw away at a banquet would feed an Indian village for a week; and the World Council of Churches or the United Nations may tell us that unless we completely reorder our priorities, hunger will become famine, and famine will become mass starvation. But if the appeal is on TV, most people will simply change channels.

If man collectively could bring himself to sufficient motivation and discipline, he could feed himself ten times over. The *Economist* makes the staggering statement that "the world's food problem has nothing to do with physical limits on food production. Even if there were no new discoveries in food-growing technology from now on, and we continued to cultivate only the very small proportion of the earth's surface now used as farmland, a raising of all other countries' efficiency of cultivation to that of the Netherlands would already suffice to feed 60 billion people." Another authority reckons that man's fundamental food requirements could be derived from 12 basic food crops. Instead, we go on eating some 80,000 edible plants. After all, life is boring enough without variety in our food menu—which brings us back to space one: only the coming again of Christ will get our 600 billion dollars' worth of annual expenditure on weapons, as we prepare for World War III, replaced with a budget that is peace-and-prosperity-oriented. Christ, and Christ alone, will turn man's swords into plowshares and his spears into pruning hooks. It really is as simple as that!

But as long as man, in the West as well as in the East, acts out that Marxist dictum that a man is what he eats, he is doomed to the consequences of materialism. It makes grim reading to look at the remainder of that passage in James 5 from which we quoted earlier in this chapter: "Listen, you rich people, weep and wail because of the misery that is coming upon you. Your wealth has rotted, and moths have eaten your clothes. Your gold and silver are corroded. Their corrosion will testify against you, and eat your flesh like fire. You have hoarded wealth in the last days" (vv. 1-3).

More attention is being paid in the 1980s to the financial state of the American and Canadian economies than in at least a generation. Millions of the young who would have gone to a university a decade ago are going to work instead. Of those who do go to a university, the *New York Times* notes that, whether it's Harvard or Stanford, many have elected to move from biology, sociology, or psychology—subjects that have been top priority—to economics, even though, as a Harvard sophomore lamented, "I hated it; I cried every night." But with the recurrent fear of recession, inflation, unemployment, and indeed of a blockbuster depression always hanging on the horizon, the young are realizing that society generally is hardening against welfarism as a life style. Kenneth Myers opines in *Time* in February, 1981, that NASA in twenty years, to explore space, did not spend as much as the U.S. Department of health and human services spends in four months. In New York 17 percent of the population is on welfare, and they know this can't go on. They realize that currently the United States economy has a public and private debt of 2.7 trillion dollars, equal to nearly $12,700 for every American. They begin to wonder whether free enterprise isn't already on the way out when of the 171 million workers in the United States in 1976, 90 million were working in government jobs and 81 million in private enterprise.

They are also strongly critical of the abuses of the system that allows 24 millionaires in the United States to pay no federal taxes whatsoever, according to Congressman Charles Vanik. The apostle Paul wrote of such capitalist abuse when he said, "in the last days" there will be "traitors" (2 Tim. 3:1,4 KJV); he also said there would be "trucebreakers" (v. 3). *Industry Week* reckons that business, through dishonesty in which employees break their promises, loses from 15 to 50 billion dollars annually, depending on who is "slicing the baloney." "Ripping off the company" is currently the common bond of both white- and blue-collar workers. Eighty-seven percent of employee crime is theft-related; most of the remainder, deliberate sabotage. All of this, added up, leads to the projection that spending for electronic security systems will grow from a billion dollars currently to two billion by 1990. One cannot escape linking this to the apostle Peter's foresight of these times: "In their greed these teachers will exploit you with stories they have made up . . . they are experts in greed" (2 Peter 2:3,14).

All of us are becoming increasingly concerned about irresponsibility. We read that during a single year the Western world's strikes and lockouts soar 35 percent, according to a report of the International Labor Organization. Some of these strikes were by such groups as teachers, and other professionals, some of whom never before were heard of to engage in strikes.

In spite of the sicknesses and disparities in the economics of the world, or perhaps because of them, there has been a definite trend toward looking more and more toward unification and a central authoritarianism in economics. The International Monetary Fund and the World Bank have been playing an even larger and more widening role in the precarious battle of balancing the international monetary movements, which at times have looked like a zigzag cardiogram after a human heart attack.

Of course, the most dramatic post-World War II development in international frontiersmanship in the economic realm (with implications leading to World War III), is the European Common Market. This body, which many Bible scholars feel is a basis for the emergent kingdom of the Antichrist (a view put forward in the film *The Omen*), currently has ten members, Greece being formally installed on January 1, 1981.

Out of ten such nations the Antichrist will arise and from this base will launch toward world conquest, until, insofar as the economic realm is concerned, he will seize a universal mandate of dictatorship that will galvanize all commerce into a centrally computerized control. Antichrist "forced everyone, small and great, rich and poor, free and slave, to receive a mark on his right hand or on his forehead, so that no one could buy or sell unless he had the mark, which is the name of the beast or the number of his name. This calls for wisdom. If anyone has insight, let him calculate the number of the beast, for it is man's number. His number is 666" (Rev. 13:16-18).

When a person with a ticket enters Disney World in Florida, he gets an identity stamp on his hand—I suppose you could have it on your forehead. It is invisible to the naked eye, but electronic scanning devices read them with total precision. Is that what Antichrist will use? In the future, credit cards or direct bank transfers will reach such sophisticated computerization that the use of money as we know it today may become obsolete. Is this the automation that Antichrist will engage?

I think any rational person would have to concede that no financial system in the world today is working for the whole world's needs. Pierre Trudeau never got such an editorial scolding since he came to the Prime Minister's office in Ottawa as when he wondered out loud if the free-enterprise system could, after all, be made to work. Then early in 1980, when in the wake of his being returned as Prime Minister, he was holidaying in Jamaica, the news report of his meeting with Michael Manley was that they had agreed that the whole world needs a new International Order if the economic inequities of our times are to be ironed out.

The ironic fact is that for the total needs of man, democracy is not adequate. Peerless historian Arnold Toynbee of Cambridge said, shortly before his death, that he was convinced of the impending "abolition of free enterprise on the economic plane of life. The economy will be put in irons." The irons will be those imposed by a dictator who may even now be lurking in the political shadows. The

Antichrist will try to impose a dictatorial economic system on all people. It won't work for long! It will lead to WW III. And the coming Christ will set up the first equitable and totally adequate economy since prefall Eden. Since the fall, man never has been able to sort out Cain's agonizing question: "Am I my brother's keeper?"

9

THE SOCIOLOGICAL SIGNS

Jesus, in depicting the scenario leading up to His return, described how society at that time will be characterized. There will be a recrudescence of the social sins and moral depravities that dominated ancient Sodom and Gomorrah in Lot's time or even the more ancient civilization of Noah's day when man had degenerated into such moral depravity that "God saw that the wickedness of man was great in the earth, and that every imagination of the thoughts of his heart was only evil continually" (Gen. 6:5 KJV). Jesus foretold that "as it was in Noah's day, so will it also be in the days of the Son of Man. People were eating and drinking, marrying wives and husbands, right up to the day Noah went into the ark, and the Flood came and destroyed them all. It will be the same as it was in Lot's day: people were eating and drinking, buying and selling, planting and building, but the day Lot left Sodom, God rained fire and brimstone from heaven and destroyed them all. It will be the same when the day comes for the Son of Man to be revealed" (Luke 17:26-30 JB).

As the Jewish pundit Mark Gayn sits in the United Nations building in New York, he ruminates that "even more dangerous than the loss of world influence has been the decline of moral standards in the West and especially in the United States." The pope feels it necessary to issue "A Declaration on Certain Sexual Ethics," a nineteen-page document that was publicized throughout the world. Noting the "unbridled exaltation of sex" through mass media, public entertainment, and even educators, some of whom "have even gone so far as to favor a licentious hedonism," the pope reaffirms that "every genital act must be within the framework of marriage." Premarital sex (which the Bible calls fornication), extramarital sex (which the Bible calls adultery), homosexuality, lesbianism, and masturbation, the pope in his Declaration insisted were always wrong. He laments that our Western society has largely degenerated into permissiveness and promiscuity. A woman wrote to Ann Landers wondering if ours has become a generation of "satyrs" and "nymphomaniacs."

The pope fingered the flood of pressures in the media and in public entertainment that militate against social and personal morality. The apostle Peter foresaw the end times as those in which men's "idea of pleasure is to carouse . . . reveling in their pleasures . . . with eyes full of adultery, they never stop sinning; they seduce the unstable" (2 Peter 2:13, 14). This is an approximate description of much that passes for theater and is shown in cinemas and on television today in film titles like these: *Girls Who Always Say "Yes!"*, *Girls of Erotica*, *The Swinging Barmaids*, *The Day of the Locust*, *Is There Sex After Marriage?* and *Confessions of a Window Cleaner*. Bob Hope currently disdains this flood of "dirty pictures. They're doing things on the screen today I wouldn't do on my honeymoon. I can't believe what they're showing on the screen. I remember the days when Hollywood was looking for new *faces*." It's what the apostle Peter prophesied would occur: an incitement for "eyes full of adultery" deliberately planned to "seduce the unstable." I commend feminist Susan Brownmiller in her *Against Our Will: Men, Women and Rape* for reasoning that "if you were to walk down 42nd Street in New York and see movie theater after movie theater showing films about the systematic gassing of Jews or the systematic lynching of blacks, you wouldn't want those theaters to stay there in the name of free speech. But you can walk down the street and see movie after movie featuring nothing but the rape and sexual humiliation of women that you'll defend in the name of freedom of speech." Susan Brownmiller and the pope are correct to remonstrate that this is the main theme of much of our public entertainment today.

Add to this the sewage that flows up out of perdition through our newsstands, causing the masses to "worship and serve the creature more than the creator" (Rom. 1:25 KJV), so that many have no eyes to see that man is reverting back to being "naked" (Rev. 3:17). Not until this last third of the twentieth century, in the long history of man, has there been such pornography as is displayed on public newsstands today. A case in point was the "Special Christmas" issue of *Penthouse*, which, in the name of that sacred celebration, published a photo sequence showing a couple having oral sex and intercourse. And when the police of Ottawa decided to ban it, the hew and cry that arose from the so-called liberal-minded vanguards of our society was astonishing. Was it any wonder that the Ottawa police should have been alarmed, since a few weeks earlier they had had to deal with one of the goriest murders in the city's history, in which a high schooler Robert Poulin raped and burned a high school classmate, shot another six students and then himself! The police found his room stacked with girlie magazines and pornographic books, the kind of which there are as many as 30 million copies sold weekly in North America. Pornography in 1981 is a two-billion-dollar industry. *Hustler* is an example of how far some magazines go. It shows *Deep Throat* film star Linda Lovelace having sex relations with a dog. Cornell College President Philip Secor is to be commended for banning *Playboy* and *Playgirl* magazines from the college bookstores.

Then there are the floods of books the pope says even "educators" are propagating, which, however sophisticated, actually "favor a licentious hedonism." President Reagan is wondering about this whole matter of sex education in the schools. He refers to the "somebody" who "decided that parents were't giving their kids enough sex education. So they decided to put it in the school curriculum. But they were so afraid of moral differences in teaching about it, they decided to teach about sex as a purely physiological act with no moral implication. The result was, sex education has been taught from an immoral view. In one school district, venereal disease among teens increased 4000 percent after one year of sex education. This is not incidental."

Then there are the sex manuals and prurient books pressed on the public: *The Sensuous Woman, The Sensuous Man, The Sensuous Couple, All You Wanted to Know About Sex But Were Afraid to Ask, The Joy of Sex,* and *The Most Fun You Can Have Without Laughing.* While some of these books may try, for the record, to skirt the matter of sex outside marriage, they certainly imply it, and no fair person could conclude that they don't produce the overwhelming effect of promoting premarital and extramarital affairs. And when a book like the admittedly fascinating (that's why it was written) *The First Time* by Anne and Karl Fleming comes out, telling how the celebrities of our times first had sex, it undisguisedly promotes the idea that prominent people as a matter of course first have sex outside of wedlock. The idolized English actress Jacqueline Bisset received accolades instead of put downs as she reckons marriage to be obsolete: "I don't know anyone who has been faithful. In fact, I don't know anyone who wants to be faithful."

Jesus warned that in the time of the end there will be seductionists who will undertake "to seduce, if it were possible, even the elect" (Mark 13:22 KJV). Another passage, dealing with people of the end times, puts it this way: "Their dreams lead them to defile the body" (Jude 8 NEB). *Time* reports a poll in which it was claimed that "984 of the 1,000 unmarried girls sampled had become pregnant listening to pop songs," the kind of pop songs that occupy "on the average of 45 percent of air time" such as: "'Do It Any Way You Wanna,' 'Let's Do It Again,' 'That's the Way I Like It,' 'I Want'a Do Something Freaky to You.'" *Time* indicates that the FCC seems to have no intention of doing much about this trend, reckoning, "Sex is so subjective. The FCC doesn't know what standard to use." If the FCC doesn't, the industry does. "At Preview House in Los Angeles, new songs are tested before a demographically selected group of 400 teenagers. As each number is played, the kids turn their dials between Very Dull and Very Good. Some seats are equipped with 'basal skin response sensors,' to measure the involuntary spasms of the nervous system. 'An orgasm sound never fails to produce a sharp spike in the BSR response,' says Larry Heller, music director of Preview House."

Surely any rational observer cannot fail to associate this kind of media pressure with what the apostle Paul prophesied to a young man: "You may as well know this too, Timothy, that in the last days it is going to be very difficult to be a Christian. For people will love only themselves and their money." Some, while "sneering at God," will be so "thoroughly bad" that they will "think nothing of immorality," to the extent that they will "worm their way into homes and gain control over weak-willed women, who are loaded down with sins and are swayed by all kinds of evil desires" (2 Tim. 3:1-3, 6). If radio and TV soap operas (a *Time* cover story is "Soap Operas: Sex and Suffering in the Afternoon") are not means engaged by a money/sex-obsessed society "to worm their way into" the desires and practices of a confused womanhood, it's baffling to figure out what they are.

Do they have their intended effect? Let's look at some indicative statistics. According to *Newsweek*, there is a dramatic increase in the "number of young teenagers seeking birth control advice . . . 15,000 girls under the age of 16 requested help from the 165 Planned Parenthood medical affiliates around the country—a 25 percent jump over the previous year . . . ten percent of the teenagers seeking counsel are 14 and under." Despite this iniquitous push to get early teenagers sexually active—for that is the effect, though certainly not always the intended effect, of pressing contraceptives onto these young girls—the latest available report is that 608,000 single teenagers in the United States became pregnant in a year. (This, in a year when the overall birthrate reached an all-time low.) In that these pregnancies produced some 407,300 illegitimate births in the United States in a year, the difference in the two figures would lead us to believe that 200,000 either got married in "shotgun weddings"—which have only a 13 percent chance of avoiding eventual divorce—or else sought and got abortions. There is hardly a more apt use of the phrase "vicious circle" conceivable.

Jesus said that prior to His return to the earth, it will be dreadful for pregnant women (Matt. 24:19). The media reports that there is a legal abortion for every four live births in the United States currently and that so-called legal abortions have increased 24 percent in a year. In Canada there has been an 11.4 percent increase in a single year to a total of 41,227, half the per capita number that took place in the United States (892,000). Anyone knows that abortion not only snuffs out the life of the fetus, but often has a tragically traumatic—if not always a physically damaging—effect on the mother and to a lesser degree on the father and all concerned, unless exercised at the discretion of a medical decision that deems the life of the mother to be in grave danger. Worldwide, the World Watch Institute calculates that the percentage of the world's population living in countries with liberal abortion laws has increased to 64 percent from 38 percent since 1970.

How many North Americans are engaging in premarital and extramarital sex? According to the latest United States census, the number of unwed couples living together skyrocketed 700 percent during the previous decade. The *New York Times* publishes the results of what is alleged to be the most thorough investigation of the American female to date. A poll of 100,000 women was taken and purports to "express the sexual attitudes, values and practices of young, middle-class, married women." This study indicates that 80 percent of the women had engaged in premarital sex (the figure went up to 90 percent for women under twenty-five) and almost half the experiences occurred at the age of seventeen or under. More than a third of the women said they had had premarital sexual experiences with from two to five men. (The Kinsey Report in 1953 found 33 percent of women under twenty-five had engaged in premarital sexual relations. So we note that in less than a generation illicit sex on the part of females has substantially more than doubled).

This polling, which was supervised by Sociologist Robert Bell of Temple University and published in the *New York Times*, indicates that 64 percent of married women engage in extramarital affairs: "Women who had never had an extramarital affair (36 percent) indicated they sometimes had a 'fairly strong' desire to do so." Of those who did have "extramarital experience, a third [had done so] with from two to five men."

Males have always been much more promiscuous than females. To accommodate those who are promiscuous there are currently an estimated half million prostitutes in the United States. They operate not merely in the old-style brothels but also in new-style body shops and massage parlors, with names like "Ecstasy Unlimited," "The Velvet Touch," and "This Is Heaven." Such places "are spreading across the country as fast as fast-food stores . . . providing 'full sexual services'" *(Time)*, and when the legal fences have to be hurdled, they change their shingle, but not what they are offering. Also spreading across the continent are "adult" motels, "adult" really being short for "adultery."

For the 5 percent of males and up to 4 percent of females *(New York Times)* who prefer homosexuality, the Gay Liberation Movement has shifted these people out of their closets, and their former shame has turned into brazen and militant aggression. Nor does it help when it is advertised that three of the National Football League's starting quarterbacks are homosexual or that gay "churches" *(sic)* are springing up in cities across the continent. No amount of rationalization will justify what God in His Word unequivocably condemns. But that it's happening is simply a fulfillment of Jude's prophecy that before the "judgment of the great day," there will be increasing numbers of people who, like those in Sodom and Gomorrah, will tire of resisting and give "themselves up to sexual immorality and perversion" (Jude 6,7 PHILLIPS); or as Paul wrote to Timothy, "in the final age of this world" men will tend to abandon "natural affection" (2 Tim. 3:3 NEB).

The situation is not helped when people in positions of leadership, having been idolized for half a generation by the peoples of the world in general and the country over which they preside in particular, are revealed to have had feet of clay, whether it's a Prime Minister McKenzie King or a Margaret Trudeau or a Princess Margaret or a Congressman Mills or a Congressman Hayes. Soloman had his 700 wives and 300 concubines, and for centuries thereafter Judah and Israel went down the same road, following his example.

Jesus said, as already quoted, that before His return, people would be "marrying wives and husbands." They are setting a torrid pace in this today. Del Fehsenfeld of "Back to the Bible Broadcast" points to "a divorce rate now reaching 55 percent. There are currently 1.2 million divorces issued each year in the United States. "In Southern California, the ratio is one divorce to one new marriage." For one year in Canada, there was a 20.6 percent increase in divorces, a 300 percent over the last decade. Massachusetts Judge Beatrice Mullaney, who had handled 10,000 divorces and separation and custody cases over a twenty-year period, fingers the Women's Liberation Movement as a major contributor to the soaring divorce rate. Even so, the United States does not lead the world in divorces. Sweden has ten divorces to every seven in the United States, to every six in England and Denmark, and every five in Russia and East Germany. Among North American Jews, divorce has risen from a rarity to nearly four in every ten marriages.

That the North American home is in serious trouble, there can be no doubt. An aspect hardly ever dealt with is the deep disillusionment with parenthood. Ann Landers astonished most of her public by her polling of parents with the question: "If you had it to do over again, would you have children?" The response was staggering. Some 70 percent of those who responded said No. She then gives some unnerving excerpts.

Even more convincing, perhaps, are the statistics of parents who are simply giving up. Tracers Company of America, the largest investigative agency in the United States, reports that women who run away from home now actually outnumber the men who do so. The New York-based company insists that a short "fifteen years ago, women running away from home in the U.S. were outnumbered by men by a ratio of 300 to one."

Judy Clabes, a syndicated columnist, points up the awful price American families are paying for mothers abdicating motherhood. Dropouts from school have increased 11 percent in three years, assaults on teachers 77 percent, and drug and alcohol offenses on school property 37 percent. The rate of armed robbery, rape, and murder by juveniles has doubled in a decade. The suicide rate for children aged fifteen to nineteen has tripled in twenty years.

And kids are getting back in other ways. For example, security specialist Edwin J. Bray, a former Chicago police detective, reveals that the latest craze of kids all over the country is to buy electronic devices for as low as $14.95 and use them to listen in on their parents' conversations. They record these conversations and play them at get-togethers. "It's really sick," he says. "Cases of kids who are bugging their families . . . are widespread throughout the country." Actually, it's an inevitable fulfillment of Paul's prediction to Timothy that society must "face the fact, the final age of this world is to be a time" when the young will be "abusive; with no respect for parents, no gratitude" (2 Tim. 3:1,2 NEB). Futurist Paul Shay in addressing the American Association for the Advancement of Science pointed to Sweden, where in 1981 "it is against the law to punish children physically or humiliate them psychologically. In fact, children have the right to "divorce" themselves from their parents."

There are other extremely painful consequences of our society's parental abdications and infidelities in addition to the incredible cost of divorce, the disastrous effects on children involved, and the already-mentioned abortion ravages. V.D., as noted elsewhere, and rape are raging out of control. Rape and its perils have had an enormous amount of press coverage recently. It is estimated that rape in one year has jumped another nine percent in the United States and 13 percent in Canada. During the last twenty years forcible rape in the United States has gone up 250 percent.

There are millions of people who realize that the world, and the West in particular, is caught up in a social sea of sex obsession, from which there seems to be no deliverance. Two hundred years ago Edward Gibbon published his *Decline and Fall of the Roman Empire*, pointing out conclusively that when ancient Rome became socially degenerate, it had no inner resources to resist collapse. Western society today is sinking down into its own sea of corruption. There is only one hope: the coming again of Jesus Christ!

10

THE CRIMINOLOGICAL SIGNS

When Jesus was asked by His disciples, "What will be the sign of your coming and of the end of the age," He replied that, among other things, there would be a dramatic and tragic "increase of wickedness" (Matt. 24:3,12). The apostle Peter prophesied that as the age reached its nadir, men would be "worse off at the end than they were at the beginning," and that "day after day," as had occurred in ancient Sodom and Gomorrah, there would be "lawless men" performing "lawless deeds" who would "follow the corrupt desire of their sinful nature and despise authority." They would act like "brute beasts, creatures of instinct," all because, within, they would be like "springs without water and mists driven by a storm" (2 Peter 2:20,7,8,12,17). One thing that is unmistakably clear in the Scriptures is that prior to the coming again of Christ, crime will run rampant and out of control. Man's laws will not be capable of controlling criminal instincts. Indeed, any rational person asks, "Can God let mankind, like an alcoholic going back to his bottle, go down into crime so far that it is no longer possible for him to live with his fellowman?" The answer to crime is Christ: His transforming power and His coming again.

Meanwhile, man's obsession with evil will become worse and worse. Paul wrote to the Thessalonians that before "the Day of the Lord" "mysterious wickedness" would obsess man (2 Thess. 2:2,7 TEV). "Mark this," Paul wrote to Timothy, "in the last days," no doubt about it, "evil men" will "go from bad to worse" (2 Tim. 3:13). In that light, *Time* reports that crime statistics are escalating in modern Israel, juvenile crime increasing in one year an alarming 37 percent.

But crime throughout the world is skyrocketing out of control. Statistics from Canada informed us that our crime went up 10.2 percent in 1980, while the *Kaya Rossiya* in Moscow in an article "Crime Triggers Soviet Campaign" laments that crime there is in places out of control altogether. In the U.S., *Time* reports a 10 percent increase in crime in 1980, Atlanta Psychiatrist Dr. Alfred Messer warning that in the eighties all the indications point to a crime increase, indubitably "headed for double digit figures." Yes, as Paul prophesied, "in the last days the times will be full of danger" (2 Tim. 3:1 PHILLIPS). "For many persons, daily life centers around the problem of safety and avoiding places perceived to be dangerous," noted the Mayor's Criminal Justice Coordinating Board of Washington, D. C. Senator Henry Jackson laments, "It's getting to be madness" when in that city, 45 percent of all women and 20 percent of all men say they never would walk out into the street alone at night. Nor is this an ungrounded fear. The FBI warns that today in America, 37 million of its citizens annually have crimes committed against them. The Gallup Poll discovers that one household in three in cities over a half million, and one in four over the whole population during the year previous, had had a burglary or a family member mugged or assaulted.

Crime currently, as the U.S. President states in his State of the Union Address, is skyrocketing. It is increasing eleven times faster than the population. In the last twenty years the number of women arrested for violent crime has increased 300 percent, women turning to crime three times faster than men. Columnist James J. Kilpatrick reckons that what should alarm Americans most is the tragic increase of crime in the suburbs, where the leaders of society live. This speaks ominously for the future. What alarms the President most is that "most crime goes unpunished": only one-third of all crimes committed are ever reported. Even more frightening is that official police reports now reveal that over the country as a whole, 79 percent of the murders, aggravated assaults, forcible rapes, robberies, burglaries, larcenies, and auto thefts that are reported and documented go unsolved. But is this getting "worse and worse"? Yes! The conviction rate for burglary since 1960 has been cut in half, and for auto theft, it decreased by two-thirds. Gregory Krohm of Virginia Polytechnic Institute, in his studies of crime, estimates that an adult burglar in the United States runs only 24 chances in 10,000 of going to jail for any single offense and that juveniles run even fewer chances. Is it any wonder that suicide among police officers is four times as high as among other people?

Crime is costly. It costs Americans an annual 60 billion dollars, according to top federal officials; 75 billion and escalating, according to *Business Week* magazine. Often, when I am asked to justify expenditures for the cost of operating a coast-to-coast weekly gospel telecast or of engaging in areawide crusades for Christ, my answer is "Yes, it costs a lot of money, but only a tiny fraction of what crime costs. Among the hundreds coming to Christ in a crusade or through a telecast, there are those who, if not Christ's, would become criminals. Currently it costs an average of $23,000 per criminal in the U.S., besides the cost to the taxpayer in apprehending him and putting him through the court process. It was calculated that it cost the FBI 5 million dollars to arrest Patty Hearst, her parents a like amount to try in vain to find her, and another 2 or 3 million to handle her through the courts—in all, 12 million dollars. And were she to serve out her initial sentence of thirty-five years in prison, it would cost another 7 million dollars, at the present rate of inflation, before she was set free.

And though most crime goes unpunished, prison building was labeled the biggest-growth industry of the seventies in the United States, with 700 jails being constructed at a cost of six billion dollars. In 1973, the State and Federal prison population of the United States stood at 195,000. Today, it is 310,000 and rocketing upwards.

Crime is especially tragic when we think of the young. In his first letter to "the young man Timothy," Paul projected that "the Spirit has explicitly said that during the last times there will be some . . . whose consciences are branded as though with a red-hot iron" (1 Tim. 4:1,2 JB). Entering the final two decades of the twentieth century, the FBI bemoans the fact that 55 percent of those charged with vehicle theft are teenagers, as are 53 percent of those charged with burglary and 49 percent of those charged with larceny! Criminologist Walter Miller of Harvard University thinks that one of the most depressing features of crime in the eighties is that currently, exclusive of murder, 75 percent of the nation's 10.2 million annual crimes are committed by persons under twenty-five and fully 45 percent by persons under eighteen. The question that is the most anguishing is this: "What does this augur for the future?"

In the matter of murder by the young, the FBI notes that during the last ten years, there has been a 60 percent increase in the number of persons under eighteen years of age arrested for murder. Ann Landers' column points up the fact that there have been over a hundred students murdered on public school grounds over the past year.

Murder is on the increase. "Understand this, that in the last days," warned Paul, "men will be . . . inhuman, implacable . . . fierce" (2 Tim. 3:1, 3 RSV). Since 1960, the murder rate in the United States has doubled. The *Stars and Stripes* reports that there are more "free-lance terrorists" killing their fellow Americans "in a month for kicks, than foreign revolutionaries kill in a year, for politics," the world over.

In Canada, murder climbs 13 percent in a year. In "Toronto the Good," it escalated 37 percent in one year. And in Philadelphia, "the City of Brotherly Love," they're rivaling Detroit that held the title for several years as "the murder capital of the world." One of the items the press notes is that if you are an American, there is one chance in 10,000 that you will be murdered this year. In Mexico it is five times as perilous, where one in every 2,000 is expected to be murdered this year, and supposedly more next year. North Americans desperately need Christ to come again, lest they kill each other off totally, like so many flies.

Already we've mentioned burglary and its shocking increases, especially among the young. Already it has gone up 24 percent in Canada. "In the last days" warned Paul "people will be lovers of themselves, lovers of money" (2 Tim. 3:1, 2; TEV, "greedy"). Theft, in one way or another, according to the president of the United States, costs that country an annual 40 billion dollars, syndicated crime costing many times more than burglary or robberies. Embezzlement, extortion, fraud, forgery, and smuggling are responsible for billions more. A University of Wisconsin professor reckons that one out of every fourteen people who enter a store shoplifts and leaves with something he or she did not come in with and does not pay for. Employees annually rob their employers of uncalculated billions. This is true in other countries of the world also—in Europe, South America, Africa, and Asia.

Jesus said that prior to His coming again and the end of the age, there would be a return to the life style that prevailed in the days of Noah: "As it was in the days of Noah, so it will be at the coming of the Son of Man" (Matt. 24:37). In Genesis we read that when God looked on the earth, at human society, He "said to Noah, 'I have determined to make an end of all flesh; for the earth is filled with violence'" (Gen. 6:13 RSV). "In the last days," declared Paul, "men will be . . . violent" (2 Tim. 3:3 TEV). Aleksandr Solzhenitsyn says one of the things that strikes him, now that he has access to the world press, is that "violence is brazenly and victoriously striding across the whole world. There was a time when violence was a means of last resort. Now it is a method of communication."

Looking at individual countries, the Russian press claims that 98 percent of Russia's crimes are crimes of violence. Here in Canada, Prime Minister Trudeau tells us that too many of us are turning into violent people. Governor-General asks us why it is that quite suddenly "Canadians are fascinated by violence" though in our history, overall, "our wilderness [was] tamed without recourse to violent acts."

In England, a poll representative of British life was taken of 1,565 youths between the ages of twelve to seventeen by Dr. William Belson of the London School of Economics. It was revealed that "nearly half of the teenage boys, selected at random from homes of all social classes in London, admit to some kind of serious violence." And even among teenage girls violence was dramatically on the increase.

Mr. Trudeau, like millions of others in North America, blames the influence of films and, more especially, television for the incredible escalation in violence. Indeed, in a special singling out of French TV in Quebec, the Prime Minister threatened that if the portrayal of violence were not sharply reduced, he would "shut down all the TV stations—or require them to show flower pots." It is a lamentable fact that throughout North America in particular, and the world in general, TV has become freighted down with the portrayal of guerilla war, skyjackings, bombings, rape, and picketings and protestings that engage violence and murders. The head of the FCC has calculated that currently by the time a child is fourteen years old, he or she has seen—on the average—14,000 killings on television. Ironically enough, children's TV shows such as "Bugs Bunny," "Pink Panther," "Speed Buggy," and "Wheelie and the Chopper Bunch" feature violence on the average every three and one half minutes. Nelson Price of the United Methodist Church's Public Media Division assesses in 1981 that "CBS's children's programs are six times more violent than its Prime Time shows; ABC is four times more violent; and NBC 2.5 more violent."

The inventor of TV, Vladimir Zworykin, was asked at the age of 87 what he thought of the current use of his invention. He replied, rather angrily, "Too much violence, too much crime. People are hypnotized by it. They look at it all the time. It is contaminating our society." When it is realized that a high school graduate has watched 17,000 hours of television, while having spent 11,000 hours in 12 years of school, on the average, then we can realize what an impact for violence TV is having on our young. This was supposed to change. But when the current TV season began, a watchdog eye noted in a *New York Times* editorial that 75 percent of the new TV programs for this season are violence-oriented. In the area of new films, it seemed tragic at the time that the film that ran away with the most Oscars was *One Flew Over the Cuckoo's Nest*. It is advertised: "Moviegoers: If violence, madness, rape, larceny, and bloodshed appeal to you, then see the best." (They might have said "the worst.") *"Dog Day Afternoon"* and *"Taxi Driver"* fall into the same category.

Joseph Kraft, syndicated Washington correspondent, reckoned in a closely reasoned article recently that all-out nuclear war is rendered more and more likely by the fact that crime and violence are insensitizing people to the perils of playing around with death instruments as if they were pawns or toys in a global game. Probably this can be seen most vividly in the fierce resistance that prevails to stringent gun-control legislation. The *New York Times* reckons that currently in the United States there are 40 million handguns, over twice the number there were when John Kennedy was assassinated. *Time* reckons that people throughout the world are selling across national boundaries 30 billion dollars' worth of killing weapons annually, made to be used in guerrilla warfare, as distinct from the current annual 600-billion-dollar armaments industry.

While violence has become "sophisticated" and the "in" thing in our society, our police, who are highly trained and, overall, highly dedicated, are suffering lower and lower esteem from the public they seek to serve and protect. "In the last days," Paul prophesied, larger and larger percentages of folk would be "abusive, disobedient to their parents, ungrateful" (2 Tim. 3:1,2). A *Los Angeles Times* polling revealed that in the last decade those who give the FBI a highly favorable rating have dropped from 84 percent to 37 percent. Who, before November 22, 1963, would ever have thought that John Kennedy, Martin Luther King, Robert Kennedy and John Lennon would die from assassins' bullets and that attempts to assassinate George Wallace and President Gerald Ford would be made.

All kinds of conscientious people have tried to rationalize crime and vindicate the actions of criminals. A well-meaning man like Chief Justice Willard Z. Estey of the Ontario Supreme Court reckons that the first step to control crime is to eliminate "the economic need for crime." An editorial in the *Toronto Star* correctly argues, "This is an old theory, but it runs directly contrary to the facts of modern experience. If it were true, a country's crime rate would fall as it became more prosperous. In Canada, exactly the opposite has happened." The problem goes deeper—much deeper. The fact of the matter is that tougher legislation and tougher courts are needed. For example, in Canada, 81 percent of the people want to return to some form of capital punishment. The government refuses. In the United States, a most recent Gallop Poll indicates that "support for the death penalty for murderers" has increased steadily over the last decade, "the percentage favoring capital punishment being currently the highest in this half of the century." It is indeed ironic that currently in North America it is much more likely that an American President or a Canadian Prime Minister will, in the course of serving his country, be put to death by an assassin, than, say, a robber who murders thirty people will be put to death by capital punishment.

Where crime has the most direct potential of exploding into World War III, however, is in the area of international terrorism, as was evident in the hijacking of an Air France jet by Arab guerrillas to Uganda and the Israelis' daring rescue of their one hundred hostages. When Brian Crozier, director of the Institute for the Study of Conflict, appeared before the United States Senate Judiciary Committee, he warned that in the area of political crime, it is all too evident that underground guerrilla terrorist groups are now preparing to bring whole cities and even nations to their knees. Crozier believes, on the basis of his network of files that "one of these days someone is going to make a homemade atom bomb. There are already thefts of fissile nuclear material." Crozier adds that such groups are planning on "attacking nuclear power stations, or stealing nuclear or chemical or biological warfare materials."

Crozier explains why terrorists are so serious a threat: "I don't think they would be deterred by anything short of total realization of their ultimate goals. I really think the whole point about terrorists is that they don't think as ordinary people do. They're fanatics. They stop at nothing. If they stop, they are not true terrorists. If they are true terrorists, they go ahead. They see it as a phase in a war to bring down a state." They are not concerned if the consequences should be WW III.

There is no other ultimate reversal to escalating crime in world society than Christ—by His transforming the individuals who make up society and by His coming again before society plunges pell-mell into universal war. The eminent authority George Wills refers to "this century of total war." One of the sure paths to WW III is the increasing callousness to crime—an attitude that is invaribly the bedfellow of war. Surely, what we need is the return of the Prince of Peace so that not only will our swords be turned into plowshares, but our gun preoccupation into gospel proclamation—until the whole human family has heard that while man brings strife and death, the God-man, Jesus, brings life and peace.

11

THE PSYCHIATRICAL SIGNS

This brings us to the psychiatrical sign of the necessity for Christ to come again soon, psychiatry being the "study and treatment of mental disease." The apostle Paul wrote to Timothy that "in the last days" on every hand there will be prominent men who will stand up against the law of God, "as Jannes and Jambres were opposed to Moses . . . whose minds do not function" (2 Tim. 3:1,8 TEV). Perhaps the foremost name in psychiatry in North America is that of Karl Menninger, who publishes a most-needed book entitled *Whatever Happened to Sin?* Relevant to our present theme, Menninger makes unmistakably clear that, essentially, modern man cannot be trusted. He suffers from too many mental disorders.

First, there is the plague of ambivalence.

Paul predicted that "in the last days people will be . . . treacherous, rash" (2 Tim. 3:1, 2, 4). At the 1981 meeting of the American Association for the Advancement of Science the American SALT negotiator, Paul Warnke, warned that man was locked into a nuclear organization called MAD (Mutually Assured Destruction). London physicist Amory Lovins reckoned "it's likely we'll all be blown up by nuclear wars in my lifetime," because moderns will likely "behave like lemmings marching mindlessly to our doom over the edge of a cliff." The only surviving American Five-Star General is Omar Bradley. At 87 he was asked what he thought man's chances for survival were, and he replied that he thought they were slim because in too many places throughout the world there are "thermonuclear giants and moral morons living within the same man." In short, there are too many leaders on the world horizon who are "treacherous" and "rash" and who, with an index finger on a nuclear trigger, cannot be trusted to restrain themselves. There is a frightening ambivalence in those people who may be geniuses and are in pivotal positions of leadership presumably for the good of others but who are totally devoid of moral responsibility: names like Idi Amin, the Ayatollah Khoumeini, and General Qaddafi spring to mind.

Mankind also suffers from sadism.

Why would man use a weapon he knows well will effect incredibly widespread destruction? Because he is suffering from sadism, a perverted cruelty. "In the last days people" will be "merciless" (2 Tim. 3:3 TEV; LB, "cruel"), wrote Paul. Ronald Pretty, in his editorial foreword to the prestigious *Jane's Weapons Systems* in writing of the terrifying laser beam weaponry that the Americans as well as the Russians have already developed to a very sophisticated stage, calls the laser beam "the death ray so beloved of generations of fiction writers." It seems incredible that man can reach such exaggerated cruelty as to want to hold a death weapon like this in his hand. But it is a prospect to be reckoned with—perhaps soon.

Man is becoming increasingly psychopathic. Paul predicted that before Christ returns people will be "brutal" (2 Tim. 3:3). The *New York Times* quotes Dr. Karl Menninger as adjudging that people today are "so desensitized to cruelty and violence that they are no longer enraged by it. Worse, they will resort to war—on any scale, because they no longer care that much." A Prime Minister of Britain has rightly warned that the real problem facing man is not the H-Bomb, but the human heart. That's what makes the bomb so ominous: man's heart cannot be trusted. In Jeremiah 17:9 we read, "The heart is deceitful above all things and desperately wicked." Man can go out and kill without conscience. The reason it is so serious today is that, except for the intervention of God, conceivably one man could kill all men. Too many men are psychopaths.

It is, of course, understandably argued that man, with his knowledge of history and his memory of World Wars I and II, Korea, Vietnam, and Yom Kippur, ought to have the sense not to go back to war. But he always has—because he suffers from *amnesia*. He forgets the past. The Bible predicts that "in the last days" men will be "fierce; they will hate the good, they will be . . . reckless" (2 Tim. 3:1, 3, 4, 13 TEV), "going from bad to worse."

For instance, what came to many as a shock, but on reflection the truth of it got through, was Malcolm Muggeridge's recent observation that "contrary to what pacifists and other humane persons would like to believe, wars, when they break out, tend to be popular. They offer the illusion of an escape from the boredom that is the lot of, particularly, technological man."

Another affliction of mankind is schizophrenia.

So severe is the human psychosis that grips many men today—some in places of key leadership—that it is not inaccurate to state that schizophrenic people have in many parts of the world climbed to the top of the human heap. These are people who, under the pressure of ethnic, economic, political, and chauvinistic stresses, and in strategic positions of power, react in a schizophrenic manner. Their neurosis builds into psychosis, and their psychosis into schizophrenia, a state in which they become dissociated from environmental responsibility and their personality responds to impulse. Certainly Hitler was schizophrenic. It is too much to hope that, apart from the grace of God, his like will not rise again. His sinister successors are perhaps even now rising to terrifying pedestals of leadership. Surely, the actions of an Idi Amin give pause to many. How the masses can respond to this kind of leadership was demonstrated by the pope's lamentation that the world's youth "are devastated by emptiness . . . and innoculated with the insanity of war." Her Majesty, Queen Elizabeth, explains how easily it happens. She notes that much "of the time we feel our lives are dominated by great impersonal forces beyond our control." Paul wrote that those who are "without self control" will bring on "terrible times in the last days" (2 Tim. 3:1,3).

Ironically enough, one of man's most dangerous traits today, insofar as his survival is concerned, is his persistent tendency to rationalize his evil. Reason, we were always taught in school, ought to save us. Instead, it is threatening to do us in by rationalization, which the psychiatrist defines as man's "attempt to make reasonable and logical any unreasonable thinking, feeling, or behavior." Take the matter of man being divided into two, perhaps three, vast armed military camps. To maintain, develop, and manufacture new weapons costs him 600 billion dollars per year—or about 1,250,000 dollars "every minute—day and night, year after year" (as a congressman declared in the American Congress). This is enough to eliminate famine from the earth: indeed, to eliminate much of the world's poverty. Of course, as long as the Soviets continue building up their arsenal, the Americans have to their's, and the Chinese their's: so goes the reasoning. As long as the Arabs are being equipped militarily by the Russians, the Israelis must be equipped by the Americans.

All men everywhere supposedly groan, "Surely there is a solution!" The Bible says it is in the coming again of Christ, for man has become self-destructing. His nuclear weaponry is a boomerang. His intent to inflict mass homicide means his own suicide. That's why the late Dwight D. Eisenhower was right when he observed that unless we have a universal moral and spiritual regeneration throughout the world, one of these days we will wake up in the dust of a thermonuclear explosion. We see now what the apostle Paul meant when he predicted that "in the last days" men with "minds warped and twisted" will be hardheaded . . . constant liars, troublemakers" (2 Tim. 3:1, 8, 3 LB). "Constant liars, troublemakers"—nowhere is this seen clearer than in today's peacemaking claims by those who, at heart, are essentially warmongers. As bells tolled in the New Year, great peace calls and claims were issued from the Kremlin in Moscow, Westminster in London, the Heavenly Gate in Peking, and the White House in Washington.

Despite the sincerity of some of these proclamations and aspirations, as Pope John Paul II points out, some of them are just so much posturing and as such are fraught with hypocrisy, for they do not lead to peace in reality. Paul wrote to the Thessalonians that they should "know very well that the day of the Lord will come like a thief in the night. While people are saying 'peace and safety,' destruction will come on them suddenly, as labor pains on a pregnant woman, and they will not escape" (1 Thess. 5:2, 3). The Vice-Premier who served as functional head of Red China said to President Gerald Ford and Henry Kissinger concerning Soviet Russia that "today it is the country which most zealously preaches peace that is the most dangerous source of war." The *Salinas Rotary Roundup* in California put it more clearly: "Countries which have the most to say about peace include the ones which start the most wars." It is well known that Marx, Lenin, and every communist leader since have exploited to the hilt the use of smoke screen peace propaganda—so much so that it is almost a service of notice that they are about to perform some new act of aggression when they come out with great peace propaganda and rhetoric of detente. No one has been more faithful to warn the West of this than Nobel Peace Prize winner and father of the Russian H-bomb, Andrei Sakharov—unless it has been Aleksandr Solzhenitsyn.

Of course, this hypocritical peace stance often reverses itself and breaks out openly into vicious vendetta, revealing a paranoia that often sounds very much like hysteria. The United Nations was established to maintain peace; yet, as former United States Ambassador Daniel Moynihan said, it seems to have descended into "a theater of the absurd," where slander, verbal abuse, invective, and heated hostilities are slung across the assembly as if it were a shooting gallery or a firing line rather than a peace palace. Linguists reckon that most of us have never really heard a war of words or the rhetoric of profane and obscene hate shots like that carried on in the United Nations, say, between Chinese and Russian communists, the Arabs and the Israelis, or the Third World delegates and nations that are thought to be racist. These word missiles certainly do nothing to promote peace. They are a further fulfillment of what the Bible says of "the last days," when men will be "grasping, boastful, arrogant and rude . . . slanderers" and verbal "savages" (2 Tim. 3:1-3 JB). Kurt Waldheim reckons that the United Nations had never found itself so ineffective as during the last few years. More and more people are wondering if its continuation is worth the effort.

Wars, explained James, are the result of a psychiatric disorder within man: "They come from your desires that battle within you" because you "want something but you don't get it." So to get it, you "kill" (James 4:1, 2). And in the end, regardless of how educated or sophisticated man is, there is no depth to which he will not stoop to get those things he feels he shuld have. The mass manic-depression that overtakes socially depressed people will, when their grievances are exacerbated enough and their hopes lifted by a band of gurus and guerrillas, cause them to go any length to realize their cravings. They may be black in a white-dominated society. They may be Irish in an Anglo-Saxon-dominated Britain. And, posing the most dangerous threat on earth, they may be PLOs in the Middle East. The apostle Paul wrote that "in the last days the times will be full of danger" (2 Tim. 3:1 Phillips), for there will be those who will be utterly "unappeasable" (v. 3 JB).

We have already discussed the perilous proliferation of nuclear weaponry throughout the world. It boggles the mind to think of what may well happen when, say, a terrorist organization such as the PLO is able to obtain fissionable material and decides to blackmail individuals, cities, or whole countries through kidnapping or hijacking. Physics Professor Tom Kibble of London University warns, "There are undoubtedly areas in the world where terrorists could hijack radioactive waste as it leaves nuclear stations. Some waste, if dispersed to the environment, would have terrible effects." Kibble believes that "terrorists could launch a form of nuclear war." The United States Atomic Energy Commission has stated that nuclear materials are definitely missing from some plants in the United States. And let it be kept in mind that it would only take forty pounds of enriched uranium or twelve pounds of plutonium to make a nuclear bomb. What's to hinder terrorists from kidnapping such a person as the MIT student who was able to devise a nuclear bomb in 222 days? Certainly, if no Western country can control the movement of such contraband poison as heroine, it would be much too much to hope that underground terrorists will never be able to get a hold of a nuclear bomb and use it to hijack and kidnap their way to their sinister ends. Terrorists tend to be the surface militants of a people in manic-depression.

With terrorists attacking from behind as big powers attack each other frontally, it is no wonder that man is sinking deeper and deeper into an anxiety syndrome. When Jesus was asked what would be characteristic of the times at His coming and the termination of the age, He replied that whole peoples "will be in anguish and perplexity" (Luke 21:25), simply "not knowing which way to turn" (NEB). Karl Menninger and his psychiatrist nephew, Dr. Roy Menninger, reckon that central to much of the social malaise and individual unhappiness of our times is the current "hopelessness in our society." Without some way "to instill hope" in the "despondent lost soul" of today's masses in general and their leadership in particular, man drifts toward the abyss of nuclear "war," a sickening, impending capitulation to a "destructive" complex from which he cannot extricate himself. Joseph Kraft, a syndicated Washington columnist, reckons that Americans have now very largely lost faith in the future of mankind. The abandonment of "faith and morale" is deep and widespread. "An attitude of caustic and corrosive skepticism has become a dominant national mood . . . from the White House through Harvard to the Chase Bank, Exxon and the Supreme Court."

Finally, with anxiety everywhere, accompanied by a dramatic drop in morale, universal man is dominated by phobias and fears of various kinds more than ever before in his long history. Jesus said that prior to His return there would be a rash of "men's hearts failing them for fear" (Luke 21:26 KJV). Heart failure has become in our time, not only the number-one killer, but the majority killer. Specialist Allan Scott states that between 1931 and 1975 "the death rate from heart disease had quadrupled," and this due chiefly to the tension, fears, and pressures of modern urban life with which man constitutionally cannot any longer adequately cope. Dr. Judith Cohen points out that after a ten-year study, she has found conclusive evidence to demonstrate that when you take people from a simple and relaxed lifestyle and plunge them into the modern American lifestyle, with all its pressures, they will "have five times their normal heart disease." Psychiatry professor at John Hopkins, Harvey Brenner publishes conclusive evidence that deaths from heart disease correlate directly with stress factors. Many people add smoking to the hypertension factor, thus forming a habit that worsens as pressures build up. Researcher Dr. Fraser Mustard states that the facts demonstrate unmistakably that deaths from heart trouble are 50 percent higher among smokers than among nonsmokers, and that this is largely accounted for by the fact that the more frightened and pressured man gets, the more he smokes. Thomas Fuller laments, "We are born crying, live complaining, and die disappointed." So we see all around us what Jesus predicted: "The beginning of sorrows" (Matt. 24:8 KJV). We realize that for too many people, life is too much, and we ask, What will give up first? Jesus said it will be the heart.

Here again is why we need Christ to come again, the Christ who told His own: "Do not let your hearts be troubled. Trust in God; trust also in Me. There are many rooms in my Father's house; otherwise, I would have told you. I am going there to prepare a place for you. And if I go and prepare a place for you, I will come back and take you to be with me that you also may be where I am" (John 14:1-3).

12

THE PSYCHICAL SIGNS

World War III, according to the Book of Revelation (16:14,16), will be detonated directly by the devil's demonization of man. Sharing that belief, Arthur Lyons, whom a high percentage of North Americans have seen on many of the TV talk shows (I saw him with Johnny Carson) has published an interesting book entitled *The Second Coming: Satanism in America* (New York: Dodd, Mead and Company, 1970).

"The Holy Spirit tells us clearly that in the last times," wrote the apostle Paul, men will be "devil-inspired" (1 Tim. 4:1 LB). To believe the Bible is to realize it is inevitable that the subject of the devil, the theme of Satan on the world scene and his ever-escalating demonization of humanity, is something of which no believer is to be ignorant (2 Cor. 2:11). Every year, every month, every day we can be sure that Satanic pollution will penetrate and saturate society more and more, until man sinks to the nadir of history in that terrible apocalyptic event of which John prophesied: "Miracle-working demons conferred with all the rulers of the world to gather them for the battle against the Lord . . . and they gathered all the armies of the world near a place called, in Hebrew, Armageddon" (Rev. 16:14, 16 LB).

Satanic mobilization for Armageddon has begun in earnest. The devil has declared war. Lucifer is on the line of scrimmage. He will not go away before Christ returns. His fury and forays on all fronts will become ever more fierce. Nauseating as the theme of demonization may seem, those who believe the Scriptures are like ostriches poking their heads into the sand if for a moment they abandon vigilance and overlook the unfolding devices of the devil, which even now can be seen to be spreading like a vast and vicious virus throughout the whole earth. We, as believers, simply have no alternative but to acknowledge the reality of our fiercest foe, ever calling on our Redeemer for His deliverance.

The devil with his demonic demonstrations has gone public in every sphere in the last few years. A generation ago, when I was growing up, Satan had a low profile. Sophisticated people generally would sooner have been caught living in a cave than admit they believed in a real, live, personal devil. But in the last decade, Satan has stepped visibly and vocally out into the open to the extent that Walter Cronkite announced on his CBS "Evening News" that belief in the existence of the devil, among Americans since John Kennedy's death, has jumped 11 percent. The Gallup Poll reveals that four times as many Americans as voted for the President of the United States in the 1980 election, affirm that they believe in a personal devil. According to the *New York Times*, there are some 200,000 practicing witches in the United States; that is, one for every thousand people.

Canadians in the 1980s are reading books and now the published diaries of our longest-presiding, late Prime Minister, William Lyon MacKenzie King, whose dabblings into the occult and the whole realm of spiritism, seances, and Satan worship come as a bit of a shock. Did he make political decisions on this basis?

What is true in North America is true throughout the world. The greatest recrudescence of Satanism, perhaps, is in Europe. In Germany, thought by many to be the most scientifically oriented and philosophically sophisticated society in history, it is currently reported that there are three million devoted devil-worshipers, and seven million sympathizers. And there are black masses being said and black magic sessions being held from Lapland to Lisbon and from Bergen to the Dardanelles.

The craze is also sweeping Great Britain, where it is said by a Member of Parliament that 78 percent of the secondary school students are, or have been, in touch with the spirit world. Indeed, there are allegedly as many witches in England currently as there are clergymen. Dr. Stephen Olford, a British Baptist, laments that as the English head into the final quarter of the twentieth century, only 2 percent are in the churches on Sunday morning, while an estimated 50 percent are involved to some degree in some form of overt Satan worship.

In Russia, notes the *Los Angeles Times*, whole villages are under the spells of witches and demons. And it is well known that South America, Africa, Asia, and the island world, all of which have had great Christian revivals, are today in the resurgent throes of a new rampant demonism. So conspicuous has Satanism become on the international scene that world publicity surrounds the Bogota, Colombia, gathering of an estimated three thousand witches, sorcerers, spiritists, and Satan-worshipers for the First World Congress on Witchcraft. Imprimatured and glamorized by conferees Edgar Mitchell, a United States astronaut, and the celebrated Jewish wizard and magician Uri Geller. Lady Sara Russell didn't make it to Bogota. The brilliant, twenty-six-year-old granddaughter of the late Bertrand Russell had gone through a Satan ritual in a Cornwall cemetery in England a few weeks earlier. Demonized, she threw kerosene over her body and, lighting a match to herself, committed suicide.

The three most prominent and influential churchmen in the world undoubtedly are the pope; the Archbishop of Canterbury; and Billy Graham. Billy Graham's views on a personal devil are well known. He believes literally and totally, and proclaims unequivocally, what the Bible says about the devil. In the controversy that arose in world Anglicanism over the existence of the devil and demonization, the Archbishop of Canterbury made it unmistakably plain that he believed in a personal devil and that wherever evil is, the devil is the initiator of it. No true effort to expose, thwart, or exorcise the devil ought to be suppressed.

And it would hardly be possible for anyone to be clearer in his statement on the devil and demons than the Pope. He grieves that Satan as a person is not only a terrible reality, but is endeavoring desperately to overpower "communities and entire societies" around the world. Pointing to the appalling and dramatic resurgence of wickedness, anarchy, and violence everywhere, the pope deplores the grievous "domination" of a large section of the human race "by Satan, the Prince of this world, the number-one enemy." He calls the devil a "terrific reality . . . mysterious and awe-inspiring." He goes on to avow that we are not merely up against it in having to do battle with Satan himself, but we are waging spiritual warfare "against an awe-striking plurality"; that is, a whole kingdom of demons commissioned by the devil.

The *New York Times*, in an article entitled "Speak of the Devil" by Professor Robet Gorham David of Columbia University, quotes one of the most influential bodies of clergy in the United States as recently affirming that "belief in the Devil is so essential a support of Christian faith that if this pillar is removed, then, of a certainty, the other parts of the structure will collapse."

With theologians recognizing the devil, a whole new wave of best-selling books has appeared on this theme. *Time* reckons that ten years ago, "it could hardly have been guessed" that a book on the devil and sorcery could "become one of the best-selling books" of recent years. Yet not only one, but several have become best sellers. In fact, two of the best sellers in the last decade in North America (other than the Bible) have been William Blatty's *Exorcist* and Richard Bach's *Jonathan Livingston Seagull*. Bach claims his book was dictated to him by the same shrill distinctive voice he would hear when, as a pilot, he would be in danger and would be given vocal instructions as to how to fly a safe course. Its success is based on Bach's taking the reader into the occult where he purportedly leaves the dimensions of time and space to ride aloft into eternity and infinity simply by utilizing his occult faculties. It is a precise inversion of the redemptive work of Christ on the cross and Jonathan Livingstone Seagull is a contrived replacement for the true Messiah, Jesus Christ.

Three best sellers that followed were books on magic by a University of Southern California scholar, Carlos Castaneda, entitled *The Teachings of Don Juan: A Yaqui Way of Knowledge*; *A Separate Reality*; and *Journey to Ixtlan*. Dennis Wheatley's novels about Satanism are airport-paperback-rack favorites.

The newsstands carry a flood of literature on the devil. A most enlightening article on this dark subject appeared in the *New York Times*, entitled "The Devil You Say" by Dr. Andrew M. Greeley of the University of Chicago. *McCall's* features "The Occult Explosion: Satan Worshippers" across America. *Time* has run four cover stories on the occult in the last decade. One was entitled "Magic and Reality," and an earlier one "The Occult Revival: Satan Returns." Of course, Satan never left. But in another sense Satan has returned in that he's out in the open again. *Esquire* throws light on the dark saga of Charles Manson and Lynette Fromme. So popular has the devil become, that whole magazines like *Voodoo* and the *Occult Trade Journal* are devoted to promoting Satanism.

Perhaps no one in industry keeps as alert an eye on where the public interest is as do the movie-makers. They turned *Rosemary's Baby* into a film of sufficient success to demonstrate that the public was ready for Satanism. So Blatty's *Exorcist* became the foremost film sensation up to its time, grossing 150 million dollars. Convinced that the market for Satanism is even lusher ahead, the makers of *The Exorcist* have produced *The Heretic*, starring Richard Burton and Oscar-winning Louise Fletcher. Meanwhile, immediately in between the blockbusters came the debauched saga of *Exorcism's Daughter, The Demons, The Devil in Mrs. Jones, Dracula, Satan's Rib, Satan is Coming, The Legions of Lucifer,* and *The Devil's Wedding Night.* In nearly any main street in the western world or almost any newspaper one can see advertised one or more of the following: *Race With the Devil, The Devil's Rain* (With the subtitle "When the Demons of Evil . . . Take All Power [and] Reason . . . Only Impulse Remains"), or *Beyond the Door* (where you're assured of encounters with "demonic possession"). The *New York Times* assures us that Satan is alive and well in modern theater" and gives a long list of plays on this theme. Is it really any wonder that the youth of our country band together under such names as "Satan's Choice," "The Devil's Disciples," "Daughters of Darkness," "Hell's Angels," or "Hell's Belles"?

In any place or age, the thinking and feeling of the youth especially are heavily determined by the lyrics and beat of its popular music. A youth analyst today reckons that one in every five songs currently has the occult and Satanism somewhere in its lyrics or its overtones or undertones. The trend began with the Blood, Sweat and Tears' "Symphony to the Devil," and The Rolling Stones' "Sympathy for the Devil." The lyrics of the latter were dedicated directly to Lucifer by Mick Jagger and became as astonishingly familiar as they are uncannily accurate in portraying how the devil works.

It could, of course, be argued that intellectuals do not take pop lyrics and film fictions very seriously. However, the movie made from the book *Rosemary's Baby* had some very serious literary thought behind it. Its author was Ira Levin, a European Jew who had seen in Nazi Germany what Paul Tillich and Reinhold Neibuhr spoke openly of as "demonic." Others of his intellectual cohorts, like Hanna Arendt in her *Banality of Evil* and Norman Cohn, became increasingly convinced that the devil was no half-comic, half-bizarre goat-man with hoofs and horn cavorting about like a satyr. He was a terrible, radically evil, and real personality. So Levin wrote about him as the spirit impregnator of Rosemary, casting him in the casual and familiar setting of an old rambling Manhattan apartment building.

C. S. Lewis and T. S. Eliot are both dead. But both blew whistles on the devil's crescendo of activity in contemporary society. Eliot in the style of Malcolm Muggeridge lamented a Western civilization "worm-eaten with liberalism," pointing to the devil's portentous "power for evil, working through human agency." Aleksandr Solzhenitsyn, in overviewing humanity as a mass, grieves openly that "demons" currently "are crawling across the whole world in front of our very eyes, infesting countries where they could not have been dreamed of" and "announcing their determination to shake and destroy civilization." In the United States, Harvard scholars Harvey Cox and John Updike were household names in the sixties; Cox for *avant-garde* social activism and Updike for sophisticated novels. Now both have written books on the devil.

Ironically enough, at this very time in our history when the teaching of the Christian faith is being driven out of our educational system, the teachings and practices of Satan and demon-worship are moving in. The fastest-growing area of study in our universities today is the field of metaphysics and parapsychology, which is an academic area heavy with the overtones not only of the whole psychic world, but also of Satan-worship and demonism. So dramatic has been this increase in interest in the occult that within a twelve-month period seventy-three American institutions of higher learning have added parapsychology to their curriculum as a major field of study. And we have lived to see many accounts of various levels of government in North America investing large sums of money in sponsoring Transcendental Meditation programs, government that has eliminated subsidies from education related to Christianity. And suddenly the United Nations, which has assiduously avoided espousal of any religion, is sponsoring T.M. programs.

Philosophers such as the late Martin Heidegger, Karl Jaspers, and the late Jean Paul Sartre seem to indicate a drift toward an acknowledgment of the personification of evil. Ruth Handa Anshen, an editor of a number of lofty humanistic publications, has written the book *The Reality of the Devil* from a philosophic point of view. She concludes with a warning: "God's way and the Devil's way part. There certainly is greatness on each side. . . . We may with certainty rely on God or on the Devil. The choice is ours."

Internationally regarded researcher Dr. Andrew Greeley of the University of Chicago writes in the *New York Times* that among the world's philosophers he sometimes "wonders whether at this stage of the game there are many left who doubt," in their moments of truth, that there is a personal devil. He goes on to concede that in the past there certainly had been a majority who had been "inclined to laugh at the Devil." They looked upon forebears who embraced the "tradition of evil spirits" and belief in Satan generally, as nothing more than people living in benighted superstition created by their ancestors, who in terms of a scientific view were little more than howling savages.

Philosophers of the recent past had affirmed that those who created a mythology of the devil were trying to cope with the mystery of evil, a mystery whose existence until very recently was denied by the modern world. There was the "problem of evil," of course, which was used in sophomore philosophy classes to prove either that God didn't exist or that His existence was at best a hypothesis. But having been used for that purpose, the problem of evil was cast aside and man continued to live in his benign, scientifically ordered universe in which human evolution and technological progress could be expected to eliminate gradually all but the barest residue of evil. Depending on whether one's prophet was Freud or Marx, one explained human evil in terms either of childhood traumas or oppressive social structures. Psychoanalysis or political revolution—or perhaps even peaceful change caused by social democracy

—could be expected to minimize the amount of evil in the world.

Such a faith was born of the Enlightenment and came to maturity in the late nineteenth century. It was struck a mortal blow in 1914 and has been dying a slow death ever since, though it stubbornly clings to life. Freudian psychology may explain the personality of Adolf Hitler, in whose web Heidegger got caught up; Lee Harvey Oswald; or Charles Manson. But it cannot explain how the evil that stems from their actions has been so vast. The net result has to be that no responsible philosopher can any longer thoughtlessly dismiss the idea of a personal devil.

If it had been suggested, say, ten years ago that the law courts in Europe and North America in the mid-seventies would begin to recognize demon-worship, witchcraft, and voodooism as factors in the commitment of crimes, it would scarcely have been believed. But it is getting to be commonplace for such a basis for conduct to come up in trials—whether in England, Germany, or the United States. Recently in England a murderer was hospitalized instead of jailed, because though otherwise he appeared to be perfectly sane, he alleged that in the moment of killing he was suddenly overwhelmed by the devil. It was a very sober instance of Flip Wilson's flip adage "The devil made me do it."

Leaders in the business and industrial communities are beginning to realize what havoc the devil can work. The *New York Times* notes that "there is a risk if you enter into business arrangements with the Devil that he may take possession." Recently, the world press carried the story of a General Electric factory in Singapore being thrown into complete chaos by an outbreak of demon demonstrations. The management, in an effort to restore normalcy, called in a witch doctor, a Buddhist monk, and an Indian mystic as exorcists to try to quell the mass hysteria that was bringing production to a screeching halt. In Toronto, a leader in commerce said that he would not like to calculate how many millions of dollars are lost annually in his city because of the antics of Satanists and the consequences of hexes struck by witchcraft on labor and management alike. Worldwide, billions of dollars exchange hands annually on the impulses provided by clues from horoscopes or impressions (or hunches) allegedly derived by ESP. A polling of Americans by a national magazine reveals that an incredible 45 percent of the people attach decision-making significance to astrology.

Millions of North Americans were both amused and amazed when the Baltimore Orioles baseball club hired a Kenyan witch doctor to put a hex on the Boston Red Sox. So the Red Sox sought help from witch Laurie Cabot to break a ten-game losing streak, and the Oakland A's owner Charlie Finley sought relief from a similar plight through an astrologer. Two years earlier, a team favored to win the World Series suddenly collapsed in the play-offs, and several players moaned, "We wuz robbed [by black magic]." A hockey team won the Stanley Cup against the odds and a "star" describes how a witch had cast a hex on the favored opposition. Many such instances could be cited. In Africa, nearly every soccer team of significance has its witch doctor. This trend is spreading to Europe, Asia, and South America.

The devil wants much more than recognition of his existence and powers in contemporary society. He wants people to be his. Some ask, "Does the devil believe in conversion?" Indeed he does. He wants people to give themselves over completely to his charge. Those who do, he strives to make over into ideal representatives of his. As the *New York Times* points out, "hundreds of thousands of witches" confess to having made "compacts with Lucifer," having "traded their immortal souls to Satan." Millions, in all walks of life, are doing just this today, some of them being in the top echelons of society. Satan prefers his disciples to appear successful.

And when someone becomes Satan's, he declares it whenever he is in society—in the home, at school, at work, in the social circle, and on the streets. Even bumper stickers are displaying the announcement: "I'm a Satan-worshiper." Elsewhere, we have noted that when the church of Jesus Christ has been raptured to heaven, the Holy Spirit's restraint on Satan's activity will be withdrawn. Satan worship will become universal, until the Antichrist, as the incarnation of the devil himself, seizes world control and demonized rulers throughout the world mobilize their armies and march them toward Armageddon: World War III.

13

THE COSMOLOGICAL SIGNS

Speaking of the ancient past, Jesus said, "I beheld Satan as lightning fall from heaven" (Luke 10:18 KJV). In Isaiah 14 and Ezekiel 28, we read the accounts of Lucifer's descent from an exalted throne in the larger universe, which he once occupied, to the depths of hell. Falling with him were the angels who became his kingdom of demons. Of the future, Jesus said, "The Son of Man will appear in the sky . . . the stars will fall from heaven, and the powers in space will be driven from their courses" (Matt. 24:29, 30 TEV). Peter enlarged on this, saying that believers "are looking forward to a new heaven and a new earth." Prior to this, "the day of the Lord will come like a thief. The heavens will disappear with a roar; the elements will be destroyed by fire, and the earth and everything in it will be laid bare. Since everything will be destroyed in this way, what kind of people ought you to be?" (2 Peter 3:14, 10, 11).

This leads us to the cosmological signs. For millennia, scientists, philosophers, and theologians have argued about whether the material cosmos—the physical universe—gradually evolved or came into existence by a sudden creative act of God.

The Bible begins with the affirmation that the universe began at some point in the past by a creative act of Almighty God. Genesis 1:1 states, "In the beginning God created the heavens and the earth."

A century ago, the consensus of scientific opinion, in the face of fierce theological opposition, was definitely inclined toward the view that the physical universe gradually evolved. Theological liberalism followed popular opinion in that direction. Then, ironically enough, it was the scientists who swung back to the biblical view, and this without reference to the Scriptures. The majority belief of the foremost astrophysicists moved back to the persuasion that the material cosmos actually came into existence suddenly. Astronomers now generally agree that the universe began with a tremendous creative explosion, which physicist George Gamou has called the "Big Bang," a view that has come to be known as "The Big-Bang Theory." It is generally accepted that the universe is some sixteen billion years old, with new estimates as discussed in the American Association for the Advancement of Science lowering this to eight billion. It is interesting that, as of 1981, Nobel Prizes have been awarded in the last four years to physicists for demonstrating the validity of "the Big Bang" theory. The earth and the other planets of the solar system are thought to be about three billion years old.

What relation does this have to the second coming of Christ and the end of the world? Fred Hoyle, Cambridge University physicist, contends (and this has become widely accepted by the world's foremost astrophysicists) that as the world and the universe at large came initially into existence by a Big Bang, so they will disintegrate and go out of existence by a Big Bang.

Dr. Paul Davies of Kings College, London, explains that all the bits and pieces of the universe will be pulled back into a dense ball when the force of Big Bang dwindles—similar to gravity pulling a rock thrown into the air back to earth. That "dense ball" may be the third heaven, the eternal abode of God. Thus, the modern physicists and Simon Peter, the ancient fisherman, say essentially the same thing: when "the day of the Lord will come the heavens will disappear with a roar," or "with a great noise" (KJV), or "with a Big Bang," as George Gamou put it. And now Fred Hoyle assures us this is the most tenable scientific position.

So, in the words of the currently popular lyric "The Outer Space Connection," man feels that he has a continuity of derivation and destiny that is not a mere up-and-down movement from dust to dust and ashes to ashes, but that someway, somehow, he is inextricably bound up with the total universe. Man inherently has a "cosmological consciousness" with which he is magnetized and through which he inherently feels a part of an infinitely greater world than the one that holds him earthbound by gravity and timebound by an ever-beckoning grave. He is the product of whoever it was who planned and made the cosmos, and his ultimate purpose in life is to discover the Way to ascend to, or indeed beyond, the stars to wherever heaven is and to make his eternal home with whoever God is. The Christian believes that "Way" is Christ!

Paul wrote about this to the Romans when he stated that "since the creation of the world God's invisible qualities—his eternal power and divine nature—have been clearly seen, being understood from what has been made." The consequence is that even those who have never heard of Christ or seen a Bible, "who do not have the law, do by nature things required by the law." But until they receive Christ, their "cosmological consciousness" remains just that—until they enter into a relationship with Jesus as Savior and Lord. Then it is that this "cosmological consciouseness" is occupied by true faith and hope in Christ. The apostle Paul speaks of this also: "Creation waits in eager expectation for the sons of God to be revealed. For the creation was subjected to frustration, not by its own choice, but by the will of the one who subjected it, in hope that the creation itself will be liberated from its bondage to decay and brought into the glorious freedom of the children of

God. We know that the whole creation has been groaning as in the pains of childbirth right up to the present time. Not only so, but we ourselves, who have the first fruits of the Spirit, groan inwardly as we wait eagerly for our adoption as sons, the redemption of our bodies [to take place at Christ's coming for his church]. For in this hope we were saved. But hope that is seen is no hope at all. Who hopes for what he already has? But if we hope for what we do not yet have, we wait for it patiently" (Rom. 1:20; 2:14; 8:19-25).

This human yearning for the coming of God down from the stars has given rise to a contagion of phenomena in this late twentieth century. As we enter the final quarter of the century, a national magazine features the fact that currently 22 percent of the American people believe in astrology (the statistic is from a Gallup poll). A Canadian professor of astronomy reckons that a third of all Canadians, at least in the world of academe, believe in, or dabble in, astrology. There are currently some five thousand Americans who make their living as astrologers. This craze has been revived because, as New York Psychiatrist Percy Ryberg puts it, "People are seeking spiritual outlets" through astrology. Increasing numbers appear "to present a reliance on something outside of this world, where we are making a mess of things."

As in ancient times, says Psychiatrist Alan Rosenberg, people have "turned in growing numbers to astrology. Frankly, I think that millions more will join the huge number already interested in astrology. They'll do it because they want to know more about themselves and more about what the future holds."

Behind it all is the fact that ours is a star-studded age. Man has looked to the stars—in Hollywood, in athletics, in the pop world, and in government—and these stars have let them down. So now they turn to the stars above and seek from horoscopes and zodiac signs and astrological charts their pathway through the labyrinth of an incomprehensible and too-often insane existence, hoping to make their eternal home in some celestial nest set up there in the stars somewhere. Even the mystery of it all adds to its magnetism.

Recently eighteen Nobel peace prize winners, as part of a prominent panel of 186 scientists, felt that something should be done about the astrology craze, which is spreading over North America in particular and the world in general. Spearheaded by the former president of the American Astronomical Society, Professor Bart J. Bok, this august body deplored the quackery of astrology that exploits the fact that people everywhere "are confused and they [the panel] are contending that these 'charlatans' traded on man's innate craving to believe in a destiny predetermined by astral forces beyond their control"—a hoped-for "future . . . in the stars." It was pointed out that 1,230 of the 1,500 daily newspapers in the United States carry an astrology column and that the latest vogue in academe was for universities to incorporate credit courses on astrology into their curricula to accommodate the current recrudescence of this ancient superstition. The panel deplored the fact that an "acceptance of astrology pervades modern society. We are especially disturbed by the continued uncritical dissemination of astrological charts, forecasts, and horoscopes by the media and by papers, magazines, and book publishers. This can only contribute to the growth of irrationalism and obscurantism. We believe the time has come to challenge, directly and forcefully, the pretentious claims of astrological charlatans . . . that the forces exerted by stars and planets at the moment of birth can in any way shape our futures."

A Canadian professor, who was one of the signatories, thought it was especially tragic that the millions who are being deceived have hung their "destiny" on "natal astrology [which] . . . holds that the directions of the sun, moon and planets in the sky, as seen from the earth at the time and place of an individual's birth," is thereafter all-pervasive in that person's life—forever.

As a believer in Christ as revealed in the Bible, I agree with the points this panel makes. The Christian's destiny is not fixed by his first birth but by his being "born again," and he is ensured thereby an entrance into the everlasting "kingdom of God" (John 3:3). This swings, not on a positioning of a star or sun in the heavens, but on the positioning of the Bright and Morning Star, Jesus the Son of God, on a Roman cross on earth; not between two candles in a cathedral, but between two thieves also on crosses; and scarcely on a gilded mountain, but on what was probably Jerusalem's ancient dump heap.

The apostle John put it this way: "How great is the love the Father has lavished on us, that we should be called children of God! And that is what we are! The reason the world does not know us is that it did not know him. Dear friends, now we are the children of God, and what we will be, has not yet been made known. But we know that when he appears, we shall be like him, for we shall see him as he is. Everyone who has this hope in him purifies himself, just as he is pure" (1 John 3:2, 3).

14

THE PHILOSOPHICAL SIGNS

The apostle Paul wrote that "there will be terrible times in the last days," characterized philosophically by people "always learning but never able to acknowledge the truth. Just as Jannes and Jambres opposed Moses, so also these men oppose the truth—men of depraved minds, who, as far as the faith is concerned, are rejected. But they will not get very far because, as in the case of those men, their folly will be clear to everyone" (2 Tim. 3:1, 7-9). So Paul, who was himself a philosopher of considerable stature in the ancient world, cautioned, "See to it that no one takes you captive through hollow and deceptive philosophy, which depends on human tradition and the basic principles of this world rather than on Christ" (Col. 2:8).

The world of thinking people today is shot through with meaninglessness. In the words of the late Bertrand Russell, "The best that we can hope for is unyielding despair." Man is physically perched on the edge of a nuclear precipice. He is in a perilous balancing act and is seized with a dizzying desperation to steady himself. At the same time he feels the strong pull toward extinction. Inundated with mountainous stockpiles of knowledge, his basic ideas about life have been exhausted. He is like the mainspring of an old-fashioned clock that is almost unwound. His oil wells of intellectual satisfaction have run dry. His psychic energy reserves have been depleted. His aesthetic horizons have leveled. Emotionally, he is saturated. Existence to modern man is like ashes in the wind. Life has been shorn of meaning. As the aging Victor Frankl pointed out recently in Toronto, "meaninglessness" is the ichabod that hangs like a terrible smog over our society. Another recent visitor to Toronto, Malcolm Muggeridge, the former editor of Britain's *Punch* and Rector of the University of Edinburgh, pronounces a feisty commentary on our times: "It has become abundantly clear in the second half of the twentieth century that Western man has decided to abolish himself. Having wearied of the struggle to be himself, he has created his own boredom out of his own affluence, his own impotence out of his own erotomania, his vulnerability out of his own strength; himself blowing the trumpet that brings the walls of his own city tumbling down . . . until at last, having educated himself into imbecility, and polluted and drugged himself into stupefaction, he keels over, a weary, battered old brontosaurus, and becomes extinct."

The *New York Times Book Review* covers two typical current works on philosophy: E. M. Cioran's *Trouble With Being Born* and Edmond Jabe's *Book of Questions*, both written initially in French. The reviewer observes that both philosophers are "sick with the problem of the Absent God, and their writings are documents about this state." Cioran makes the judgment that "a book is a postponed suicide." Jabe, in a spirit of gloom, writes, "Knowledge itself can be defined as detailed awareness of unsolved problems." The reviewer concludes that, as with most of today's philosophy books, "the only pleasure to be derived from reading these two books is the satisfaction of total despair."

People's confidence in institutions has plunged to such a low that if this despair sinks much lower, one wonders how much longer they can continue to function. In 1966, 42 percent of Americans had a great deal of confidence in

Congress; currently it is 9 percent. In medicine, in 1966, it was 73 percent; currently, 42 percent. Higher education has plunged from 61 percent to 31 percent; the military from 62 percent to 23 percent; the press from 29 percent to 20 percent; the presidency from 41 percent to 11 percent.

Politicians feel this philosophic pull toward nihilism. We could quote pivotal people in Britain, the United States, or Russia, like Governor Brown of California, who, during his brief stint at seeking the Democratic candidacy insisted that today's mood is to tell people, "You're going to be sick and have heartaches; you're going to die." Perhaps quotations from a couple of Canadians are relevant here. George Beverly Shea and I spent part of a December afternoon with the late Prime Minister John Diefenbaker. The eighty-year-old Diefenbaker told us that Canada "is a country without a soul—a people lost in frustration, and a leadership that will not lift them up." What he might have added was that the only leader who can really lift us up is the Lord of Glory, who will also, one of these days, lift his believers to heaven. Then there is former Postmaster General Bryce Mackasey, who laments that the gloom of our generation is largely the result of the destruction of beliefs and values: "Keynes destroyed our belief in the discipline of money. Freud destroyed our belief in sexual discipline. Dr. Spock almost destroyed our belief in discipline for children. Einstein destroyed the discipline of absolute values. We gave up the goal of heaven for heaven on earth." In short, because man philosophically wanted to replace the coming of Christ to take us to heaven, with the coming of man to the garden of ease, he has lost all anchorages and thrown his compass into the sea. Adrift in a dark night of gloom, he has the terrible gut feeling that he has gone by the harbor of heaven and, now adrift, is headed for hell.

Meanwhile, as Mackasey points out, he is throwing his ideals, so costly in their purchase over the last five hundred years, right down the drain.

The late Albert Camus wrote that suicide is the essential moral question of the twentieth century. In the third quarter of this century, suicide among 15-to-24-year-olds (the time of life when philosophic idealism runs highest) has trebled in North America, and, as the late Bishop Fulton Sheen in an address before his death stated, during the two years previous, suicide among youths under eighteen years of age had actually doubled. *Homemakers* report that in Canada since mid-1974 suicide among teenagers has trebled. Suicide in the United States went up 25 percent among all ages in a single year, the biggest jump in twelve months in this century. That year 25,000 college and university students attempted suicide. Many, when they read statistics like that, will wonder why man, a four-and-a-half-billion population mass, doesn't collectively agree to annihilate himself with thermonuclear weaponry, rather than charge toward the same goal by exterminating himself one by one, life becoming simply too much for him to cope with any longer.

The entertainment world today is filled with philosophic despair. David Bowie, the pop idol, has been quoted in the *Rolling Stone* for what has come to be a fashionable confession, almost a status-symbol statement: "I'm very, very bored." Phil Ochs, who collaborated with Bob Dylan in the protest lyrics of the late 1960s, hangs himself rather than turn to Christ as Dylan has. Ochs's "Talking Vietnam" led to "I Declare the War Is Over" and "Cross My Heart, I Hope to Live." But alas, hope and life gave way to his tying a rope around his own neck, for, as someone explained, "Phil had been very depressed for a long time." Add to this a Freddie Prinze, a Sid Viscious, a Barbara Hutton, and now a Tim Hardin at 39 and the only son of 1981 Golden Globe winner Mary Tyler Moore.

Then there's Paul Simon, who makes a comeback to express his despair. The *New York Times* characterized his Columbia release "Still Crazy After All These Years" as "an eloquent expression of adult despair." Paul Simon has never been able to cross his own "Bridge Over Troubled Waters." Youth search for a drop of refreshing reality in Simon but find themselves sorting in vain "through his lyrics like ancient priests rummaging through the bones of dead birds, arranging and re-arranging in a search for hidden messages." It's all devoid of uplift; there is only "moody, gloomy imagery." You sense a terrifying pattern of desperation when you hear of Tom Jones complaining that though he lived the happy, simple life of a Welsh laboring family, now he enjoys "beautiful sunshine, the plush hotels, the exotic meals" and life "gets almost unbearable"; and when you read of another Welshman, Antony Armstrong-Jones, crying amidst the shambles of a long-gone marriage to Princess Margaret: "I am desperately sad"; and yet another Welshman, Richard Burton, lamenting, "How can I cure myself of the agony and idiocy of this strange world!"

Of Canadian Joni Mitchell's "blue" album, Peter Goddard notes that you can sense that she herself believes she epitomizes Western man as "a lady in a Paris dress with runs in her nylons." Her "sense of unease runs through everything." You cannot escape feeling "her restlessness, her need for travel." All men have this yen to "travel"—especially, though they may not know it, they want to "travel" to heaven, but that can happen only if Christ comes to get us. In Hebrews 4:1; 9:28 we read that believers have the sure "promise of entering His rest," because for those who so prepare, Christ "will appear a second time, not to bear sin, but to bring salvation to those who are waiting for Him."

And lest this despair be thought of as a youth kick, in vogue for the young alone to admit to, it might be well to quote Red Skelton, who languishes today as "a recluse." He is described by his friends as being "one of Hollywood's loneliest men, tormented by insecurities, troubled by insomnia, plagued by a phobia about phones." Wouldn't it be wonderful if Red Skelton were to get a call from Christ telling him that He is coming back—soon—and that he should prepare to meet Him? The fact is that Jesus Christ has put in such a call to him and to the whole human race. But we must answer that call. The apostle Paul wrote to Timothy, "Take hold of the eternal life to which you were called" (1 Tim. 6:12).

And philosophic despair is in the schools, where, the Bible predicts, in the last days men would acquire stockpiles of knowledge but be unable to apply them to the hard realities of life (2 Tim. 3:1, 7). Professor of International Affairs at the University of Toronto, Dr. James Eayres, reckons that "there is a malaise abroad in the academy, a sickness of the spirit." It affects all intellectual echelons to the extent that generally "teachers have lost the respect of their students, are losing respect for themselves. They are deeply divided on what they should be teaching, more deeply still on how." Dr. Eayres concludes, "The university is no longer a place of light, liberty and learning . . . only a place of loneliness." The president of the University of Toronto, Dr. John Evans explains, "Until a few years ago it was commonly accepted by academics that through research most of the major problems of society could be solved," but "at the end of the 1960s, it was recognized that most of these problems weren't solved." No, "they were still there. And in fact they were getting bigger." Toronto educator Loyd Howse reckons that "the malaise that pervades" colleges and universities today is "that we are virtually leaderless."

And it is just here that the danger lies. The worldwide intellectual community has endeavored, by and large, to reject belief in God. Among the mentors of the intellectuals has been the late Julian Huxley, who arrogated, "God is no longer, among others, a useful hypothesis. A faint trace of God still broods over the world, like the smile of a cheshire cat, but psychological science will rub even that form from the universe." That did not happen. Psychological science is not a savior. So the schools, which already have been inundated by gurus on their campuses, have developed a huge vacuum that is waiting to be filled by a leader.

Paul wrote to the Thessalonians that Christ will take His own—from all professions, nations, and generations —home to heaven, and then on this earth "the lawless one [the Antichrist] will be revealed." This "coming of the lawless one will be in accordance with the work of Satan displayed in all kinds of counterfeit miracles, signs and wonders, and in every sort of evil that deceives those who are perishing. They perish because they refused to love the truth and so be saved. For this reason God sends them a powerful delusion so that they will believe the lie and so that all will be condemned who have not believed the truth but have delighted in wickedness" (2 Thess. 2:8-11).

Daniel said that the Antichrist will "speak great words against the Most High" (Dan. 7:25). He will not "regard the God of his fathers" (Dan. 11:37), since he "opposeth and exalteth himself above all that is called God" (2 Thess. 2:4).

Certainly one of academe's predominant traits of the last generation has been its increasing disposition to embrace atheism. This has not been generally true of scientists. At the end of World War II, a third of American scientists reportedly believe in God; now the number is two-thirds. But the philosophers, the literary people, and the educators, whose derivation, institutionally as well as intellectually, has been from the church, have made a concerted effort to go atheistic. So teaching basics about God from the Bible in the schools has been illegalized in the United States in the wake of crusading by such antagonists of believers in a personal God as Madalyn Murray O'Hare. It is refreshing to hear President Reagan state that for too long "Atheism, which in fact is a religion, has been favored over the godly faith that has built America. The Constitution says we are a nation under God." He resolves to reverse the trend that has favored those who "have created almost a religion of their own in that belief [atheism] and are demanding things for their religion that they would deny others."

An atheistic philosophy is always an extremely dangerous one, because it invites, or rather, demands, a god-figure to fill the vacuum. A case in point was the late Martin Heidegger, who at the time of his death was described by the late Jean Paul Sartre as "one of the greatest and most creative philosophers of the twentieth century." It was Heidegger who took Soren Kierkegaard's existentialism and adapted it into his own "atheistic existentialism." However, when

Hitler came along, Heidegger shocked and angered his philosopher contemporaries by joining the Nazi party in 1933 and siding with Hitler. Christless and godless, as Heidegger professed to be, he apparently needed a Hitler to fill the vacuum. And it was also significant that Sartre, at the time of his death in 1980, had lost interest in living, his doctors unable to diagnose why he died, except that he had lost the will to live. He was a manic depressive: something that sprang from his "God is dead" contention, and something that was tragically evident in his novels *Mausea*, his play *Exit*, and his tract *Being and Nothingness*.

Ironically enough, Sartre in the last years of his life was a Maoist. Mao Tse-tung made athiests—if that's possible —out of more humans than anyone who ever lived. Yet Mao, asked at the time of his eightieth birthday what he intended to do with the rest of his life, allegedly assured, "Prepare to meet my God!" So whether a person's name is Henry Kissinger or even Mao Tse-tung, regardless of what his ideological posturing may be, he cannot ever really get God out of his mind.

Many think of Joyce Carol Oates as contemporary America's foremost philosopher/novelist. Her masterpiece, *The Assassins*, features a philosophical conservative, Andrew Petrie—a sort of composite of James and William F. Buckley—as an ex-senator who edits a national review. He's shot while in temporary retirement, writing a book on how to save civilization by forming an international network of supermen.

The Assassins has three sections, giving three versions of the meaning of Petrie's life from people closely involved in his fate: his two brothers, who deplore his politics, and his widow, who believes he's an important philosopher. Brother Hugh Petrie is a savage political cartoonist with a nihilistic vision. His attempt to seduce Andrew's widow, Yvonne, is a last grab at life—his brother's life. He ends by botching his suicide. Yvonne is a woman who lived to propagate Andrew's ideas, but in the end she is hacked to death near the place where Andrew was shot.

It is Stephen, the younger brother, who makes the work of Oates so very reflective of consummation philosophy. He turns to God and in total commitment feels he has found a key to the future. Faulty and incomplete though Oates' description of a true Christian may be, it is certainly indicative of "the God who is there."

We are living in a time when thinking people have to turn one way or the other. For the masses, as one writer laments, it is a matter of "drinking as if there is no tomorrow." But responsible people today must have the mind-set of the futurist. There is, for example, a very select all-Canadian club denominated "Gamma," an elitist eclectic group made up of some of the best brains in the country, concentrating as a "futurist study group." As *McLean's* magazine comments, our world today witnesses "a North America gone seminar-mad with endless conferences on the future of Mankind!"

One philosopher who has settled his account with his Maker and has had a very profound impact on the intellectual life of our time throughout the world is Francis Schaeffer. He had been brought up in a liberal Protestant church and, hearing no answers to life's basic questions, he abandoned the church to become an agnostic. But wading through deep philosophic waters, ancient and modern, he found no formula for life. The whole matter of human existence was to him an unresolved riddle.

He entered into a six-month period of deep quest. Picking up a Bible, he began to read short passages at first, but those lengthened into a serious search. The search did not end in more searching, as Buddha's search did, but in a finding—a finding of the truth, that Truth being an experience of Jesus Christ as Savior and Lord.

Through Schaeffer's research center at L'Abri in Switzerland, from which has issued a stream of thoroughly intellectual treatises on theology and contemporary philosophy, his movement has done more to channel the minds of our generation intellectually toward a true preparation to meet our God than perhaps any other movement of our time. The point needs to be made here that frequently—too frequently—Christians tend to play philosophical fashion games, by implying that knowledge of Christ's sure coming again is not really very important. The apostle Paul, in introducing perhaps the most familiar passage in the Bible on the second coming of Christ, exhorts in regard to this theme: "Brothers, we do not want you to be ignorant" (1 Thess. 4:13).

15

THE ECCLESIASTICAL SIGNS

We have already noted that one of the biggest and most pathetic news stories in the late 1970s was the earthquake which struck Guatemala one February morning. Twenty-two thousand people were killed, a million left homeless.

That very morning, the *New York Times* came out with an article by an assistant professor of English who was also an ecclesiastic. Covering the top half of the page across from the editorials, the article entitled "Doomsday Is Coming at 7:32 A.M., January 20, 2000 (6:32 A.M. Central Standard Time)" circulated throughout the continent and elsewhere in the world. Ironically enough, as it ridiculed "Evangelical authors" who point to "earthquake and death that will precede Jesus' just and merciful return," it appeared on the very day that the hemisphere's second most killing natural disaster to date was to take place. The author made several fallacious or grossly exaggerated statements; for example, "Evangelical authors" teach that "by 2000 each person will be confined to one square foot of land." This, of course, is a statement that could only have been made by someone who was at that moment talking like a lunatic, not a true evangelical.

But the real rub was that the writer identified himself with "church builders," who teach that "Jesus is a God of love and hope with a determination to improve man's plight on earth by hard work and social change." He concludes, "Our civilization must seek to renew itself"; that is, it must not expect a divine intervention. This is humanism, not Christianity. The author takes his most satirical swipe at a sign he saw by the roadside in the American South: "Watch—King Jesus Is Coming Soon."

Now with an article like that in mind, let us look at a paragraph in 2 Peter 3:3-7, which reads, "First of all, you must understand that in the last days scoffers will come, scoffing and following their own evil desires. They will say, 'Where is the "coming" He promised? Ever since our fathers died, everything goes on as it has since the beginning of creation.' But they deliberately forget that long ago by God's word the heavens existed and the earth was formed out of water and with water. By water also the world of that time was deluged and destroyed. By the same word the present heavens and earth are reserved for fire, being kept for the day of judgment and destruction of ungodly men." Peter assures us that "the day of the Lord will come like a thief. The heavens will disappear with a roar; the elements will be destroyed by fire, and the earth and everything in it will be laid bare (v. 10).

The author of the *New York Times* article was right indeed in pointing to the folly of date-setters—of the past and future—for the advent of Christ. Jesus clearly said that no one but the Father knows when it will be (see Matt. 24:36). But to dismiss with satire the biblically assured return of Jesus Christ to this earth, and to do it as a "church builder" who believes "Jesus is a God of love and hope" and at a time when the whole flow of current events worldwide is in the direction of the extermination of both the visible church and man himself is to go in the opposite direction of scriptural teaching. Yet, as we've pointed out, such an attitude was predicted by peter, whom the church universal believes was an apostle, a teacher, and a revelator of God's Word for His whole church to follow.

This leads us into the thesis of this chapter: that a sizeable percentage of the visible, professing church worldwide will, in the last quarter of the twentieth century, look at the massive biblical teaching on the second coming of Christ, repeat weekly the creeds of the church, all of which include direct and unmistakable reference to His return, sing hymns to this effect and be totally immersed in the traditional profession of this doctrine, and yet, when pressed, will come right out openly and deny vociferously that they have any belief whatsoever in the literal, personal coming again of Jesus Christ. Astonishing as that may be, it's true! And it's a direct fulfillment of New Testament prophecy.

We have quoted from the apostle Peter. Paul also wrote of end-time unbelief. He taught that in the last days people will be lovers of themselves, "having a form of godliness, but denying its power." Then he warns, "Have nothing to do with them" (2 Tim. 3:1-5). And again, "The Spirit clearly says that in later times some will abandon the faith and follow deceiving . . . teachings" (1 Tim. 4:1, 2). "If you point these things out to the brothers," Paul says, "you will be a good minister of Christ Jesus, brought up in the truth of the faith and of the good teaching that you have followed" (1 Tim. 4:6). Here Paul is dealing with people within the organized church. John also prophesied of such a posture among church people previous to the return of Christ: "To the angel of the church in Laodicea write: . . . You are neither cold nor hot . . . because you are lukewarm—neither hot nor cold—I am about to spit you out of my mouth. You say, 'I am rich; I have acquired wealth and do not need a thing.' But you do not realize that you are wretched, pitiful, poor, blind and naked . . . buy from me . . . white clothes to wear, so you can cover your shameful nakedness" (Rev. 3:14-18).

In Toronto a theatrical group, financed by the tax-supported Canada Council, Ontario Arts Council, and Metro-Toronto, presents the following scenes in a church sanctuary, with the minister in attendance: nudes performing a do-it-yourself abortion, a lesbian being raped by motorcyclists, an amateur in a brothel, and other scenes too distasteful to mention here—all with a heavy mix of obscenities and profanities. Nor was this a one-night stand. It was held nightly from Wednesdays to Sundays for 12 weeks and reportedly attracted 12,385 people, understandably with full coverage from the media. Across North America currently, there are increasing numbers of churches with openly "homosexual ministers" (*sic*) who are being ordained by mainstream denominations and these actually are reported to "marry homosexuals and lesbians to each other." In Texas the press reported that a "church stripper stripped before children." Just how strong the ground swell of infidelity in the church is—and it is present in all mainline denominations—can be demonstrated by how much flak Pope John Paul is obliged to take repeatedly when he issues his strong, biblically sound stands on the matters of fornication, adultery, and homosexuality. The tidal wave of protest from around the world and from within the church reaches near-hysterical proportions in some places.

And to move from the voice of St. Peter's Cathedral back again to the apostle Peter in his speaking of the dark last days leading up to the time when "the day dawns and the morning star rises," we read that bold and arrogant people will come with "boastful words, and by appealing to the lustful desires of sinful human nature, they entice people who are just escaping from those who live in error. They promise them freedom, while they themselves are slaves of depravity—for a man is a slave to whatever has mastered him. If they have escaped the corruption of the world by knowing our Lord and Savior Jesus Christ and are again entangled in it and overcome, they are worse off at the end than they were at the beginning. It would have been better for them not to have known the way of righteousness, than to have known it and then to turn their backs on the sacred commandment that was passed on to them. Of them the proverbs are true: 'A dog returns to its vomit,' and 'A sow that is washed goes back to her wallowing in the mud'" (2 Peter 1:19; 2:18-22).

People who enter the church and then leave, or stay in and live a farcical rather than a forceful life of testimony to Christ, tend to lapse first in conduct and then in doctrine. To rationalize their degraded life style, they will often stay in the church and twist its doctrines in an effort to justify their actions. I am acquainted with a world-famous English bishop who says frankly, despite the fact that Jesus said, "You must be born again"; "Count me among the once-born men." And his attitude toward moral standards, as taught in the Ten Commandments, is much more unchristian than that of many atheists. "People today," writes another well-known churchman, "have no interest in the emotionalism of the cross and Christ's shed blood." This could hardly be more accurately prophesied than in 2 Peter 2:1, 2, where we read that in the last days there will be false prophets among the people, just as there will be false teachers" who "introduce destructive heresies, even denying the sovereign Lord who bought them—bringing swift destruction on themselves. Many will follow their shameful ways and will bring the way of truth into disrepute." A prominent minister tells an assembly of clergymen of Canada's largest denomination that the day of telling people how they ought to behave is over: "Some see God as a kind of divine rapist who wants to force his passion or love into us." That surely is blasphemy.

So it's really no wonder that apostasy has been taking over whole sections of the church and driving the people out into a pagan vacuum. The Scriptures predict such a falling away. Paul wrote to the Thessalonians that in the last days "the coming of our Lord Jesus Christ" will be preceded by a "falling away first" (2 Thess. 2:1,3 KJV). This "falling away" can be seen in the liberal church in the United States, where 1974 proved to be the first year in the two-hundred-year history of the United States that total church membership actually decreased (by 180,000). *Time* reports that since 1966 the United Methodist Church, the United Presbyterian and Episcopal churches, and the United Church of Christ have lost a total of 2.4 million members. These are the denominations that have given the largest espousal to liberal and radical theology. And in the later seventies they continue to lose ground, though the rapid overall evangelical growth has caused the church statistics to swing up again. In the latest Canadian sensus count there were ten times as many Canadians who registered their religious affiliation as "none" as there were ten years previously. A CBS-TV national newscast claims that a polling of the Canadian people reveals that in one generation the percentage who went regularly to a place of worship had been halved. According to a BBC poll of the people of Britain only 29 percent—down 18 percent in a decade—believed strongly that there is a personal God. Jude warned that "in the last time there will be scoffers who will follow their own ungodly desires. These are the men who divide you, who follow mere natural instincts and do not have the Spirit" (Jude 18,19). *Time* states that the "Big Five" elitist seminaries of American Protestantism (Harvard, Yale, Chicago, Vanderbilt, and New York's Union Theological Seminary) have abandoned their former basic required courses in the Bible and in church history and that there's been a "radical decline in chapel attendance at seminaries . . . manners are more relaxed, sex freer, and acquaintance with drugs often more than theoretical." These, laments *Time,* are tomorrow's ministers.

To Timothy, in his final recorded chapter, Paul wrote that prior to Christ's "appearing and his kingdom . . . .the time will come when they will not endure sound doctrine; but after their own lusts shall they heap to themselves teachers, having itching ears; and they shall turn away their ears from the truth, and shall be turned unto fables" (2 Tim. 4:1-4 KJV). No reasonable number of pages pointing to fulfillments to these prophecies would begin to demonstrate how precise these predictions have proven to be in today's world. In the realm of cults, there have been great advances in Spiritism, Mormonism, and Jehovah's Witnesses, the *Toronto Star* fingering the last-named as "the fastest-growing religious group in Canada and, possibly, the world," its membership having already doubled in the 1970s.

One of the movements of our century within the Christian mainstream, which began with lofty aims and aspirations, is the ecumenical movement. Springing from a vigorous and even euphoric nineteenth-century evangelicalism, it liberalized and even radicalized its theology during the first three quarters of this century to the extent that today its official stance has tended more and more toward syncretism than apostolic Christianity. In the 1910 Edinburgh World Missionary Conference, an event that sprang directly from nineteenth-century revivalistic and evangelistic movements, especially those in which D. L. Moody took the lead, the emphasis was on world evangelism. By the time the World Council of Churches had emerged from this base in 1948 and had gone from Amsterdam to Evanston (1954), to New Delhi (1961), to Uppsala (1968), and to Nairobi (1975), the theology of the Council represented the liberal wings of the major denominations. A few years ago, Visser't Hooft, who was for the most of its existence the Secretary-General of the World Council of Churches, characterized the movement in *Time*, as one where "confusion reigns supreme—politically, theologically, socially," admittedly a rather strong statement.

Throughout the world of the eighties, the press treats the council usually as more interested in left-wing political movements than evangelism, in social revolution than in spiritual regeneration, and quite often in backing left-wing guerrilla uprisings than in freedom of religious expression.

In an account on a WCC meeting, the *Toronto Star* stated that many of the delegates "vehemently insisted that it [the meeting of the WCC] was a fundamental betrayal of the Christian gospel." Religion editor, Anglican Tom Harpur, wrote, "Any attempt to raise the specific issue of religious or political freedom in Soviet-bloc nations seemed to be constantly thwarted." He pointed to the fact that many disillusioned "delegates are confused over what it all has meant and frustrated by the way in which the assembly was conducted [by] a core of 'old boys.'"

But really, some say, this sort of thing doesn't have much clout in the political arena. On the contrary, it has enough that the churchmen who represented its posture emerged at the head of the communist MPLA (popular movement) in Angola, which, armed by the Soviets and with Castro's 12,000 soldiers at the fore, took over Angola. Not many weeks had passed before the regime was reportedly putting greatly added pressure on evangelical Christians to silence their witness.

The political stance that some in the WCC today are adopting is one that points to a future of which Hiley H. Ward in his *Religion 2101 A.D.* (1976) projects:

> The church—that spired building on the corner—will have disappeared almost completely. Roman Catholics and the familiar Protestant sects—Methodists, Baptists, Presbyterians—will be only 'remnant groups,' with a few diehards holding on to the old-time religion. The mass population will have gone on to a huge, wholly ecumenical religion sanctioned by the state. Christian theology is likely to be watered down with Jesus as only one of several savior figures who are accorded spiritual significance . . . Jesus-like symbols [will] drift into the American religious outlook—from the Eastern religions. God might come out more as a computer, or some other concept, rather than a man on the ceiling of the Sistine Chapel . . . the separate doctrines and rites of traditional religions will be of virtually no importance, even though some of the rites may be continued, like baptism and communion.

With this in mind, let us turn to Matthew 13 and the words of Jesus in which He taught that "the kingdom of heaven is like a man who sowed good seed in his field. But while everyone was sleeping, his enemy came and sowed weeds among the wheat, and went away. When the wheat sprouted and formed heads, then the weeds also appeared."

So the workers asked the owner, "'Do you want us to go and pull them up?' 'No!' he answered, 'because while you are pulling the weeds, you may root up the wheat with them. Let both grow together until the harvest.'" Jesus explained, "The one who sowed the good seed is the Son of Man. The field is the world, and the good seed stands for the sons of the kingdom. The weeds are the sons of the evil one, and the enemy who sows them is the devil. The harvest is the end of the age. . . . The Son of Man will send out his angels, and they will weed out of his kingdom everything that causes sin and all who do evil. They will throw them into the fiery furnace, where there will be weeping and grinding of teeth. Then the righteous will shine like the sun in the kingdom of their Father. He who has ears, let him hear" (Matt. 13:24-29, 37-43).

The contention of the New Testament is that in the field of the visible church are two concurrent crops: the wheat, which Jesus states plainly are those who are His, and the weeds, which are planted in darkness by the devil. Often they are visibly indistinguishable, and, as Jesus states clearly, for us as spiritual husbandmen to try to totally weed out sons of the devil is not only not our job, but we may tear up the whole field of evangelism in the process if we try to do so.

One day—perhaps soon—Christ will come again, and His angels will "gather together" His own to bring to Him. Many of those inside as well as those outside the organized church will be left behind. When all of the born-again believers in Christ—Catholic, Orthodox, Protestant, and unaffiliated—have gone and what Jesus called the "great tribulation unequaled from the beginning of the world until now, and never to be equaled again" (Matt. 24:21) takes over, what will become of the organized remnants and mainstreams of the church? They will all merge into one monolithic ecumenical religious organization and since hundreds of millions of saints who had saving faith in Christ will have been raptured home to heaven, this superchurch will become the haven of hundreds of millions of others who will seek spiritual security in it. With the Holy Spirit no longer restraining the mystery of iniquity, this ecumenical ecclesiastical amalgam will quickly take shape. In autumn of 1979 occurred a Conference of Christians (sic), Buddhists, Confucianists, Hindus, Jews, Janists, Moslems, Sikks, Shintoists, and Zoroastians uniting in New Jersey to form their "Princeton Declaration of the World Conference on Religion." This is the sort of amalgam which will evolve rapidly into the ecclesiastical Babylon we read of in Revelation 17 and 18.

Being in alliance with the political powers of the Middle East, this supra-religious organization will work in concert with the emerging Antichrist. This unholy bedfellow arrangement is pictured in Revelation 17, which describes an evil harlot riding a scarlet-colored beast. For centuries, Bible scholars have been convinced of this significance: the harlot is a religious monster-movement, and the beast is the Antichrist. This wicked marriage will be the phalanx of a world sinking to an all-time nadir of immorality. Only the return of the Creator-Redeemer Jesus will be able to restore righteousness and correction to a degenerated world. Is it any wonder that the Bible draws to a conclusion with the cry of the aged apostle John, who had foreseen visions of all of this and heard the final testimony of Christ when He said, "Yes, I am coming soon! John exclaimed in response, 'Amen. Come, Lord Jesus'" (Rev. 22:20).

On the other hand, while liberalism has stifled and shrunk the sections of the organized church worldwide wherever its withering influence has been embraced, the story of the Evangelical church worldwide is a complete contrast. It is currently flourishing vigorously.

In Acts 2:17, 21 we read the promise: "In the last days, God says, I will pour out my Spirit on all people. Your sons and daughters will prophesy, your young men will see visions, and your old men will dream dreams. . . . And everyone who calls on the name of the Lord will be saved." In the following chapter (vv. 19,20) Peter reiterated: "Repent, then, and turn to God, so that your sins may be wiped out, that times of refreshing may come from the Lord, and

155

that He may send the Christ, who has been appointed for you—even Jesus." James clearly exhorted that we are to be expectant of "the Lord's coming." Of the "fall and spring rains," the latter is a signal that "the Lord's coming is near." As the early church had an outpouring of the Holy Spirit, so the coming of Christ is to be preceded by another great outpouring of His Spirit.

A 1980 Gallup Poll indicates that 52 percent of Americans say they have had a "born again" experience, an increase of 30 percent in 18 years. And Americans are encouraged by a 1981 Gallup Poll which reveals that church membership has increased 1 percent—to 69 percent—in the last year.

It was an unprecedented thing for a president to say in his Inauguration address, what Ronald Reagan stated on January 20, 1981: "I'm told that tens of thousands of prayer meetings are being held today. I am deeply grateful. I suggest that today and that this day hereafter should be declared a Day of Prayer."

It is interesting, as Russell Chandler of the *Los Angeles Times* points out that the only presidential candidates who seem to interest the public enough for them to gain widespread support were those with an evangelical conversion and such a life-controlling experience of conversion that they were willing to talk about it. He cited Jimmy Carter, Ronald Regan, and John Anderson, who, by late May were the only serious contenders left in the presidential race. Chandler went so far as to contend that for the first time in American history the single most important thing about a presidential candidate the last two times around, as far as the American people were concerned, was his faith. Chandler proved to be right both times.

In Canada a CBC-TV national newscast states that a poll reveals that the Canadian people want their clergy to get back to the biblical basics and preach a "conservative" message from an "evangelical" point of view. It also stated that currently wherever this position is proclaimed, there is rapid growth.

Another indicator of the upsurge in interest in Christianity has been the best sellers, *The Living Bible* having outsold all other books in the United States in the last ten years, current sales topping 20 million.

According to the *New York Times*, in a single year there has been an astounding 23.6-percent increase in religious book sales, the evangelical titles being far in the lead in popularity.

Outside North America, there has never been a greater spiritual harvest. Billy Graham declared in Albert Hall, London, in January 1981 that throughout the world there are 50,000 being born again daily, and there are a thousand new churches being opened weekly. In South America, where I've recently been, evangelicals are increasing currently at a rate of approximately 15 percent per year. In Africa south of the Sahara, it is even greater, and in much of East and Southeast Asia—e.g., in Indonesia and South Korea—it is reportedly four times as rapid as the population growth. Jesus promised, "And this gospel of the kingdom will be preached in the whole world as a testimony to all nations, and then the end will come" (Matt. 24:14).

Currently the Canadian Bible Society reports that portions of the Scriptures are appearing in a new language every thirteen days. Scriptures now have been published in languages spoken by 97 percent of the people of the world. The last fifth of the twentieth century began with a year in which 25 million complete Bibles were distributed throughout the world. Wherever the written Word goes, there goes the Word of Life to all who believe.

16

THE HISTORICAL SIGNS

William Buckley entitled one of his "Firing Line" programs on coast-to-coast TV "Israel: Headed for a Messianic or Catastrophic End?" One hundred million Arabs are committed to the "catastrophic end" for their 3.5 million Israeli neighbors. The Israelis themselves, as Ben-Gurion their first Prime Minister often said, believe they have actually returned to await the coming of their Messiah. As Israel celebrated her twenty-fifth anniversary of nationhood after 2,500 years of being either occupied or dispersed, the head rabbi of Jerusalem told the world that Jewry was now a sovereign state, an earthly kingdom among other kingdoms. But in the future, he said, the Messiah would come and reign over the whole world from Jerusalem, just as the prophet Micah foresaw (Micah 4). There is a universal realization that something really ultimate and definitive is currently happening in the Middle East. Americans apparently believe this, to the tune, as their former vice-president affirms, of giving half of their foreign aid to this tiny nation (a mere 3 million of the earth's 4.5 billion population).

Charles Malik (Ph.D., Harvard), the Lebanese statesman who served as past president of the United Nations

General Assembly, said before the current chaos into which his country has fallen—a happening that renders his judgment that much more significant—"To dismiss the present conflict between the children of Isaac and of Ishmael [the Israelis and the Arabs] as just an ordinary politico-economic struggle is to have no sense whatsoever of the holy and ultimate in history."

The *sine qua non* of scriptural prophecy is the people of Israel. Increase Mather was president of Harvard from 1685 to 1701. In *Mystery of Israel's Salvation Explained*, written at a time when Palestine was a desolate wilderness in the hands of the Turks and virtually completely devoid of Jews, Mather wrote with regard to the regathering of Israel to their ancient homeland that "the Scripture is very clear and full in this, that you see not how it can be justly denied or questioned." Mather foresaw that "the Israelites at their return shall even fly," basing this assumption on Isaiah 31:5, "as birds flying." Anyone who has recently been to Israel cannot escape seeing this happen on six out of seven days in Tel Aviv airport. John Owen, a foremost English Congregationalist, wrote in 1673: "The Jews shall be gathered from all parts of the earth where they now are scattered, and brought home into their homeland." An anthology of such statements during every generation from A.D. 70 to the present could be written.

Why should Israel, whose world numbers are 14.15 million (only one-half of 1 percent of the world's population), be the special object of the Lord's regathering? Because God keeps His promises. In Genesis we read that God said to His friend Abraham: "Get thee out of thy country, and from thy kindred, and from thy father's house, unto a land that I will shew thee: and I will make of thee a great nation" (Gen. 12:1, 2). When Abraham had obeyed God and left Ur of the Chaldees and had gone into the land that is modern Israel, God again spoke to him and said, "I will give unto thee, and to thy seed after thee, the land wherein thou art a stranger, all the land of Canaan, for an everlasting possession; and I will be their God" (17:8).

Moreover, in speaking of the covenant He would make with Abraham's seed, He said, "I will bless them that bless thee, and curse him that curseth thee" (Gen. 12:3). That the Jewish people are the recipients of these promises was later indicated by the Lord's reappearance to Abraham to assure him, "In Isaac shall thy seed be called" (21:12). For 430 years, Israel sojourned in the land of Egypt until Moses and Joshua guided them back. Later, during the times of the kings, there was apostasy; so Israel went into Babylonian captivity, but Nehemiah and Ezra led them back again.

In an Israel that had been occupied by foreign powers since Nebuchadnezzar's siege in 486 B.C., our Lord was born of a Hebrew virgin. A third of a century later, having come "to that which was his own" and having been rejected by his own (John 1:11), He was crucified. During the week of our Lord's crucifixion He predicted, "All these things shall come upon this generation." This was unmistakably the siege and utter destruction of Jerusalem by Titus of Rome in A.D. 70 in which Jews were massacred and those who escaped fled to the ends of the earth, a scattering from which they have only begun to return during recent years. Jesus made it plain: "They will fall by the sword and will be taken as prisoners to all the nations. Jerusalem will be trampled on by the Gentiles until the times of the Gentiles are fulfilled" (Luke 21:24). When it is realized that Jerusalem has been a city occupied ever since by Gentiles until the Six-Day War in June, 1967, it is evident that we are living in very exciting times indeed.

Meanwhile, from the time Peter was mandated to take the gospel to the Gentiles by going to Cornelius and his household, the church of Jesus Christ has been constituted chiefly of non-Jewish Christians. James argued to the Jerusalem Assembly (Acts 15:14-16), "Simon has described to us how God at first showed His concern by taking from the Gentiles a people for himself. The words of the prophets are in agreement with this, as it is written: 'After this I will return and rebuild the fallen house of David. Its ruins I will rebuild, and I will restore it.'"

In Paul's letter to the Romans, chapters 9 to 11 are strikingly relevant today. In the Acts of the Apostles it is made plain that because the Jews had rejected the Lord of glory and the gospel message, God had turned to the Gentiles to regenerate a body of believers known as the church. Paul's teaching reiterates that fact: "Through their [Israel's] fall, salvation is come to the Gentiles." But this, he states, is a parenthesis. He cautions Gentile believers that they are wild branches grafted into the true tree of God's chosen but that as Israel has been set aside so shall she be taken up again: "You will say then, 'Branches were broken off so that I could be grafted in.' Granted. But they were broken off because of unbelief, and you stand by faith. Do not be arrogant, but be afraid. For if God did not spare the natural branches, He will not spare you either" (Rom. 11:19-21).

Paul goes on to say that "God is able to graft them in again. After all, if you were cut out of an olive tree . . . how much more readily will these, the natural branches, be grafted in to their own olive tree?" (Rom. 11:23, 24). Summing up, Paul clarifies, "There is a deep truth here, my brothers, of which I want you to take account, so that you may not be complacent about your own discernment: this partial blindness has come upon Israel only until the Gentiles have been admitted in full strength; when that has happened, the whole of Israel will be saved." Concluding, Paul declares, "God's choice stands, and they [Israel] are his friends for the sake of the patriarchs" (Abraham, Isaac, and Jacob) (Rom. 11:25, 26, 28 NEB).

The prediction is clear, and the immense amount of Old Testament prophecy pertaining to the final restoration of Israel to their ancient homeland becomes astonishingly meaningful. For example, Isaiah, who devoted whole chapters to this theme, is the Lord's oracle of prophecy: "In that day the Lord will reach out his hand a second time to reclaim the remnant that is left of his people . . . from the four corners of the earth" and "they will possess the land forever" (Isa. 11:11, 12; 60:21).

Three points here: "Again" can only refer to a regathering of Israel since scriptural days, because the regathering from Babylonian captivity was the only other one from Isaiah's time to this. "To reclaim the remnant . . . from the four quarters of the earth"—or as Jeremiah 32:37 puts it, "Behold, I will gather them out of all countries, whither I have driven them in mine anger"—can only refer realistically to the current return of Israel, because any previous dispersions were merely to one or a few nations in the Middle East, certainly not to anything like the "all countries" in "the four corners of the earth." Modern Jews have returned to Israel from 107 countries literally all over the world. As one observer once said, you can find Jews and Coca-Cola nearly anywhere in the world. In China, the most populous country in history, only a score or so Jews remain; half are about to be ejected, and the other half, it is reported, are aged or infirm and will soon die.

A second point: The most amazing migration of Jews to Israel in our time is from the Soviet Union, where the first three of Israel's five prime ministers were born. In any one year currently, it is incredible that as many Jews get out of the Soviet Union to emigrate to Israel as all other emigrants from Russia to all other countries of the world combined. That in itself is a miracle. All of this is not, of course, achieved without an enormous amount of lobbying around the world, creating pressures that even the Soviet system finds difficult to resist. For example, we see world Jewry assembles delegates in Brussels for a World Conference on Soviet Jewry, its one predecessor in 1971 having resulted in an unprecedented wave of Jews returning from Russia to their ancient homeland, Israel.

The third point is this: "Thy people shall inherit the land for ever." "I will bring back the captivity of my people," as Amos puts it, "and they shall no more be plucked up out of their land which I have given them, saith Jehovah thy God" (Amos 9:14, 15 ASV). This indicates that Israel will not be "driven into the sea" as the surrounding nations say so often. Nor will Jerusalem again become a part of a Gentile empire. This was underscored when the world press carried the stunning revelation that Israel now has her own supply of readied nuclear weaponry.

The fact arises that Israelis are moved to return to their land by nationalist and ethnic ties as much as by an attachment to Judaism. This is precisely as the Scriptures predict: "Afterward shall the children of Israel return, and seek the Lord their God, and David their king" (Hosea 3:5). The sequence is that they would return to their ancient homeland, largely in unbelief, as Paul taught, and, when settled, would await their Messiah. At the revelation of Jesus Christ, a "nation will be born in a day," and as W. A. Criswell, former President of the Southern Baptist Convention in the U.S., declared at the Jerusalem Conference on Bible Prophecy, there would be realized the "happy prospect" that Israel will "repent over her rejection of the One she pierced, the Lord Jesus Christ." When our Lord was about to be born, His coming was to witness "the falling and rising of many in Israel" (Luke 2:34). Note the order. Israel would "fall" and be scattered but they would "rise" again. Typical titles for histories of other nations read, "Rise and Fall . . .," but for Israel it would be a "Fall and Rise." Throughout the world today, Jews are on the rise, despite efforts to put them down. For example, of the 32,000 scientists in the Soviet Union with Ph.D.'s, 4,200 are Jewish, sixteen times as great a proportion of Jews as in a cross section of Russian society.

Turning to a précis of events pertaining to Israel's restoration, such a volume of evidence has been accumulating over the last few years at such a pace that the phenomenon almost staggers an objective observer. I happened to be preaching in The People's Church, Toronto, on the Sunday night in June 1967 when rumblings of the "Six-Day War" indicated that the Middle East was breaking into flames. As Levi Eshkol, then Israel Prime Minister, pointed out, Israel could only get scattered snatches of arms (their tanks were World War I vintage and apparently obsolete). They were outnumberedd forty to one by Arabs whose armies were outfitted with Russia's best and who repeatedly had resolved to drive them into the Mediterranean. In the teeth of these overwhelming odds, I read on that occasion Luke 21:24 in which Jesus stated that when God's time for the return of Christ was drawing nigh, Jerusalem would no longer be trodden down by non-Jews. On the basis of Jesus' statement, I intimated that it would not surprise any Bible believer if within hours the Israelis were again in possession of Jerusalem, never again to be expelled. In a matter of six days, this and much more was history. The geographical size of Israel was suddenly quadrupled. *Time* pointed out that the repossession of Old Jerusalem by Israel was a fulfillment of a biblical prophecy that had to occur before the second coming of Christ, a fact that the last four, if not five, U.S. presidents have agreed is a tenet of the prophetic Scriptures. One of President Reagan's first resolves was: "First, I believe that this nation has a moral obligation and commitment to the preservation of the nation of Israel."

It was my honor to appear on a Canadian television network program, "Perry's Probe," with Dr. Case, President of the Association of Orthodox Jewish Scientists in Canada. Asked if, as a scholar, he believed in miracles, Dr. Case went into careful detail to point out that the whole existence and expansion of the modern state of Israel has to be a miracle. There simply is no other explanation for it.

The Bible predicted that Jews would be "hated of all nations." How else can you explain Hitler's extermination of some six million Jews? Aleksandr Solzhenitsyn astounded the world recently by revealing that Stalin's death could best be explained by stating that it was a direct judgment on him for his newly contrived plan systematically to slaughter, if possible, all Jews in Russia, having already exterminated some seven million.

The *Miami Herald* points to the fact that there has been a strange and inexplicable "disappearance" of more than 100,000 Jews from the Soviet Union over a ten-year period. Senator Claiborne Pell asks why the half million Jews in Moscow are permitted only one rabbi. The late Prime Minister John Diefenbaker of Canada asked why the only reporter who was denied a visa to go to Russia with Pierre Trudeau was a Jew.

We, the Billy Graham Team, feel so strongly the wrong of atrocities against the Jews that two of our main films have been *His Land*, about Israel, and *The Hiding Place*, which depicts how the Dutch sisters Corrie and Betsy ten Boom exercised their Christian love in Holland during World War II by giving themselves to rescuing and preserving Jews from the Nazi Gestapo. For doing so, Betsy and her aged father were put to death in a very cruel manner.

One of my Jewish neighbors said to me one day: "Everyone is out to get us. Why us?" When "Miss Israel" was chosen "Miss Universe 1977," she stated that her aim would be to cultivate friendly relations with her Arab nation neighbors throughout the Middle East. One of her rivals in the Miss Universe pageant told me personally of how difficult a task that would be. Look at the vote in the United Nations. Only three times in my memory has it been lopsided in the extreme. In 1956, when the Israeli-Egyptian crisis arose, 71 countries voted against Israel; one, for. When in 1967 the United Nations voted on whether Israel should retain possession of Jerusalem, which they regained after the Six-Day War, the vote was 69 against, none for. When Arab commandos slew two Jews at the Athens airport and Israel retaliated by destroying thirty planes in Lebanon on the basis that a man is worth more than many sparrows (even if they are huge metal ones), the Athens incident never got to the United Nations officially at all, but the Lebanon affair did, even though not a single life was lost. Israel was outvoted 101 to nil.

Late in 1975, a resolution was passed in the United Nations that astonished millions throughout the world. It contended that Zionism, the Jewish National movement, is actually "racism and racial discrimination." The "Zionism Earthquake," as it came to be known, drew a hue and cry of protest from Jews throughout the world and also from many non-Jews who, in the interests of fairness, contended that this was a gross miscarriage of justice. In Canada, Roman Catholic and Protestant churchmen jointly issued a statement that this resolution was not only immoral, it was a gross denial of the United Nations charter. Editorialized the *Toronto Star*, "The real target of the Arab-Soviet lobby is the destruction of the State of Israel." Said Andrei Sakharov, father of the Russian H-bomb: in the 1980s, "The Soviet Union has raised anti-Semitism to the level of religion in a godless society."

Within two months Dr. Nahum Goldmann, President of the World Jewish Congress, lamented that relations "between Israel and the non-Jewish world are fast deteriorating; the honeymoon between Israel and the non-Jewish world has come to an end." Rabbi Plaut, Canada's leading Jewish spokesman editorialized in the *Toronto Globe and Mail* that whatever Israel "does, with the best of intentions, is considered wrong." It's a matter of being "hated of all nations." Is it any wonder that 6 billion of Israel's 18-billion-dollar budget is earmarked for defense? As of this writing, in 1981, there is a militant move afoot by the forty-two-nation Arab Alliance to have Israel put out of the United Nations altogether.

And the Christian church has much too often offended the Jewish people. Remember the unfortunate instance in 1980 when an evangelical leader said God cannot answer the prayers of Jews. And despite ecumenicists' ironic overtures, Rabbi Emil Fackenheim reflects that many Christian denominations are more antagonistic toward Jews today than they have ever been in history. Evidence of this could be seen early in 1981, when four-hundred liberal American churchmen, including several bishops, petitioned the American government to reduce aid to Israel and begin giving support to the PLO.

What makes the Israeli state more miraculous is the fact that never in history has a country gone out of existence and come back into existence after a burial of even 500 years, let alone 2,000. A hundred and thirty years ago, Jerusalem had a population of 3,000 Jews; and all Palestine,

8,000. Seventy years ago, there were still only 41,000 Jews in Palestine, and even after World War II, only half a million.

Today there are three and a half million, and with ample land in their possession and as one of the six nations on earth that produces more food than their home market consumes, there is now plenty of room for a rapid increase in population. One has to see Israel to believe that this land, until recently a barren wilderness, is such a flourishing garden today. Rabbi Yosef Derman of Toronto points proudly to the fact that, in 1948 the Palestinians had only 85,000 acres under cultivation, today they alone have 195,000. Agricultural output has been increased 60 percent in Israel in one generation, this apart from the additional occupied areas, where not only agricultural output has been multiplied, but substantial oil resources have been discovered. In the words of the prophet Ezekiel, as he interprets that valley-of-dry-bones parable (given such worldwide publicity in a pop song before the Russian premier when he was entertained in the United States by the president): "This land that was desolate is become like the garden of Eden; and the waste and desolate and ruined cities are become fenced, and are inhabited" (Ezek. 36:35). As Jan Smuts, a giant among twentieth-century statesmen, commented, "The greatest miracle of the mid-twentieth century is not the invention of thermonuclear devices, but the return to their ancient homeland of the Jewish people" precisely in fulfillment of biblical prediction.

The fact that the Jews would migrate back to Palestine, with the scriptural conviction that this was inevitable, came very much to the fore among Protestant theologians in the nineteenth century. This paved the way for the political possibilities. Simultaneously, Jews all over the world were fascinated by Theodor Herzl's Zionist Movement, which sought to stir support for a restoration of Palestine to homing Jews. In 1917, General Allenby of Britain captured Jerusalem from the Turks without firing a shot, and in November of that year, the Balfour Declaration made it possible for the Jewish people to settle unharassed (theoretically, at least) in their ancient homeland. It is interesting that the eminent Jewish scientist, Albert Einstein, and theologian Martin Buber were for many years dead set against a Zionism that promoted a return of Jews to Israel. Before they died, both were passionate devotees of the State of Israel.

In October 1947, there was a sufficient sense of equity on the part of the great powers to lead them to try to compensate Israel for what Nazi Germany had done. Support was rallied in the United Nations to give Israel a charter to become a sovereign and independent state. The land allotted was slight, but as the hundred million Arabs ganged up to nip the flower in the bud by demolishing Israel, the first of four miracle-fraught skirmishes took place in which Israel not only survived, but expanded.

So it has happened since, and so it will surely happen again. I was in Egypt on a day when the late President Nasser exclaimed that another war with Israel was both imperative and "inevitable." The *Chicago Tribune* refers to the Jewish/Arab conflict as "irreconcilable." As I am writing, thirty-seven of the forty-two Moslem nations are met in Saudi Arabia, resolved to: "urge the United States and other Western nations to refrain from helping Israel in any fashion; urge member nations of the United Nations to freeze Israel's membership, thereby barring the Jewish nation from all U.N. activities; use all the Islamic states' military, political, economic, and natural resources—including oil—as an effective means."

The scriptures teach clearly that the Middle East conflict cannot be settled, and will not be settled, until Jesus Christ comes again. As *Newsweek* puts it, the Middle East is that "perennial chestnut."

"The Bible," asserted the late David Ben-Gurion, "is our mandate." It is not insignificant that the former Prime Minister of Israel gave the opening speech to the Jerusalem Conference on Bible Prophecy, other speakers being evangelicals. Newsman George Cornell notes, "In Italy, it's the opera. In Switzerland, it's the Alps. In Russia, it's the Party. In America, it's baseball. But in Israel, it's the Bible. It's the people's principal pastime." They search its pages for guidance in every detail for the restoration of "the land." Joshua Cohen writes in the *Toronto Star* as a Jew: that "what the world in general and Israel in particular today needs is not basically a materialist solution to their problems: guns and money don't always save countries, empires or people. Our Bible saved us; could still save the world too, if it followed the Bible. Try it."

Modern Israel has only one three-hundredth of the population that modern China has, yet this tiny nation gets three times the headlines around the world. Why? Because it is the hinge country on which the world swings. History began in the Middle East and it will end there. There is no point at which Scriptural prediction and current events so exactly coincide as on this Jewish issue. The newspapers are replete with it. Whether you read the headlines, the editorials, letters to the editor, religion or the financial page, statements abound such as in the *Toronto Star* in which it is declared that this little land has "expanded beyond pre-1967 Israel's wildest dreams." Jewish people have a fierce love and allegiance for Israel, wherever they may live in the world; whenever opposition to their cause arises, they close ranks rapidly. *Time* quotes Israel's leaders as wanting a million more workers immediately. And while other nations want to reduce their population growth, Israel is working on doubling hers in the next decade.

I shall never forget arriving in Jerusalem on the eve of the first New Year the Israelis were in occupation and sovereign control of their capital, since two and a half millenniums ago. I have never felt such electric expectation. The air teemed with it. Crowds rejoicing and weeping for joy were everywhere. The exhilaration on the faces of gathering Jews resembled that of little children as they tear open their Christmas parcels on the morning of the 25th of December in our country. The Ram's horn was ready to blast out the sound that Messiah had come. The old wailing wall, newly excavated and bared down seventeen stone levels, was the scene of indescribable festivities and anticipation! I felt that until that moment, like most Christians, I was unable to grasp what power there is in revived and expectant Judaism. If it is asked whether or not Israel will relinquish Jerusalem again to any other power, the answer of the Prime Minister is: "Absolutely, absolutely not."

Even interest in a restoration of the temple is now quickening. The *Washington Post* on May 21, immediately prior to the Six-Day War when Old Jerusalem was taken, ran an astonishing quarter-page advertisement entitled, "TO PERSONS OF THE JEWISH FAITH ALL OVER THE WORLD." It stated, "A Project to Rebuild the Temple of God in Israel is now being started. With Divine Guidance and Help, the 'Temple' will be completed. It will signal a new era in Judaism. Jews will be inspired to conduct themselves in such a moral way that our Maker will see fit to pay us a visit here on earth. . . . Executive talent, administrators, and workers on all levels are needed. . . . God will know those desiring to participate." A box number was given. Eventually, according to Moshe Dayan, there will be an extension of Israel's "frontiers to where they belong" to include all "the land between the Nile and the Euphrates." Did Dayan not demonstrate in 1967 that his predictions were as substantial as Nasser's were empty? There is an inevitability about modern Israel.

The Israelis themselves are more and more coming to believe that they are back in their homeland to await the coming of Messiah. Christians rejoice in this, believing that the expected Messiah is indeed Jesus Christ. Ben-Gurion and Levi Eshkol, Golda Meir, Yitzhak Rabin and Menachin Begin have all affirmed frequently that modern Israelis are returning to await the advent of Messiah. Before his death Joe Pyne, radio-television probist, interviewed a Jewish Rabbi. Mr. Pyne asked the Rabbi about Israel's real reason for being back in "the land." Without hesitation, the Rabbi replied that it was to await "the coming of the Messiah." Some people are not aware that one of two lyricists who wrote the rock opera *Jesus Christ, Superstar* was a young English Jew. No, he does not get Jesus Christ up from the dead, but he does bring Judas back. And the question asked again and again is one that Jews will more and more be asking: "Jesus Christ, Superstar, are You really who You say You are?" The question is repeated over and over again: "Who are You? What have You sacrificed?"

Meanwhile, the words of the greatest Jewish Christian since Christ, the apostle Paul, ring out: "I am not ashamed of the gospel, because it is the power of God for the salvation of everyone who believes: first for the Jew, then for the Gentile" (Rom. 1:16). Until Christ comes to take His church home, it is our task to win all people in general, but in particular, Jewish people, to Christ. In the most recent report from the "Jews-for-Jesus" movement, headquartered in San Rafael, California, it is stated that more than 14,000 Jewish people have made personal commitment to Jesus as Savior and Messiah in the last decade in the United States, others claiming this figure could go as high as 100,000. Sid Roth, the Jewish evangelist, told me early in 1981, that the last few years have been the first in two thousand in which more Jewish people, on an average worldwide, than Gentiles are turning to Christ. Surely this is indicative of the spiritual "latter rain," indicative that Christ's coming again is getting ever closer.

In the Revelation of Jesus Christ we read that during the Great Tribulation period on earth, there will be 144,000 Jewish Christians evangelizing the world and giving their lifeblood for their Lord. Meanwhile, today there are great Jewish evangelists. Perhaps the greatest sermon I've ever heard or read on the second coming of Christ was one by Dr. Hyman Appleman. Dr. Appleman was a Jew, born in Russia and brought up in orthodox Judaism. An immigrant to Chicago, he became a brilliant lawyer. He mastered the Old Testament Scriptures and believed in the coming of the Messiah, but somehow he couldn't put it together. There was something missing. That missing something was Someone—Jesus the Son of God. When Dr. Appleman experienced Christ in the new birth and Holy Spirit power, he realized that Messiah Jesus had already come, and was coming again. This transformed not only his life, but the lives of tens of thousands of those to whom he preached.

17

THE POLITICAL SIGNS

The Club of Rome has issued this proclamation: "The governments and international organizations of today are obsessed with military alliances and bloc parties, not realizing that in the event of a nuclear war these would prove useless. The only way of escaping nuclear destruction is to try to meet together the greatest challenge which has ever confronted mankind." The scriptural prophecies with regard to the political entities, posturings, alliances, and wars of certain nations, especially as they affect Israel at "the time of the end," are so many and explicit that they simply cannot be ignored. Nor should they, when such phenomena as the regathering of Israel, their achievement of nationhood, and their seemingly incredible expansion—despite the fact that they have initiated none of the skirmishes that have resulted in their aggrandizement—have thinking people everywhere wondering.

Other honest questions are being asked, such as: Can a militantly atheistic philosophy such as Communism, which overran the world's largest country, Russia, and its most populous, China, and which strives relentlessly by any and every means to take over the whole population of the earth, persistently going as far as it dares to exterminate wittingly the faith of Jesus Christ and His church, escape the ultimate judgment of God? William Buckley reckons that we are naive and totally irresponsible to forget so soon that butchers in Russia have slaughtered 60 million dissidents, and in China, 100 million, countless numbers of these having been devout Christians. China, like the other communist countries, has many of the most dedicated believers in history, who are living under a regime that is even more hostile to Christian belief than was ancient Rome. Fifteen years ago 30 million Red Guards boasted that they had succeeded in closing every solitary Christian church. How long can that regime hope to circumvent the intervention of the God they deny? Or take the case of Cambodia, where the communist regime that took over in 1975 has, according to the *New York Times*, in seven years wiped out 3.4 of 8.9 million people. I think we will quickly agree that God's statement of judgment in Ezekiel 38, "I am against thee!" is a valid response to Communism today.

Western Europe and North America, as Victor Hugo has stressed, have, as a result of their Christian character, produced a varied orchard of the richest fruit in human history. In the wake of Christianity, civilization, culture, education, wealth, and technological advances have staggered the imagination, but the very Christianity that provided the base for all this is in eclipse. According to a recent widely publicized Gallup Poll, every single country in Western Europe simultaneously registers a distinct decline in Christian belief. As the Archbishop of Canterbury points out, we are witnessing the advent of the post-Christian era. Can such a state of affairs long escape the tyranny of an Antichrist? Especially when it is considered that, according to some, the church will be driven underground or, as in my view, it will be taken upward into heaven, withdrawn from the "wrath to come!"

Our Lord forecast that prior to His coming again there would be "wars and rumors of wars." It was not only divinely prophesied, but such leaders as Douglas MacArthur,

Dwight D. Eisenhower, leading authors, and the prestigious editorial writers of the *London Times* predict a coming Armageddon with uniform regularity. According to a standard dictionary, the meaning of Armageddon is a "place of a great and final conflict between the forces of good and evil." Will such indeed occur as World War III, as so many pivotally-placed scientists and statesmen are saying?

Is Russia in biblical prophecy? I think it is—most precisely in Ezekiel 38 and 39, also in Daniel 11 and Revelation 20. Certainly, as the leader of world Communism, Russia has been at the fore of communist-incited revolutions for a half century now, revolutions that have changed the face of the earth's political geography and the whole course of twentieth-century history. Jesus forewarned us that prior to His coming again there would be "wars and revolutions." The communization of Eastern Europe occurred as a result of the Soviets' opportunism late in World War II and the compromises the Western Allies were prepared to make with Stalin—just for peace. Within four years, nearly another one-fourth of the human race fell to the communist revolution in China. Since 1950, the Korean and Vietnam wars dragged on and on, with half of Korea and all of Vietnam—along with Laos and Cambodia going communist as Cuba did earlier. Chile and Portugal have their romances and disenchantments with Communism, as do Italy, Iran, and Zimbabwe. Ethiopia and Libya seem to be gone, with Chad and Syria keeping everyone wondering. Then we enter the eighties with the Soviets crashing into and conquering Afghanistan.

William Buckley reckons that the often ridiculed "domino theory" of communist conquest is proving to be true after all, while Henry Kissinger went so far as to say that all Western Europe will be communistic in ten years. Angola went communist, it seemed, on the very road on which the Americans withdrew from Vietnam. After all, the Russians rightly calculated, the American people wouldn't help save Angola after having withdrawn so ingloriously from Vietnam. Aleksandr Solzhenitsyn appears on British Broadcasting Corporation television and laments that he was sure the number of years that the free world would be remaining free are few, because no one really cares much anymore, and freedom has to be defended by vigilance and sacrifice. He contends that the Russians use "detente" as a chess board, to which they've got especially the Americans to pull up their chairs and play. Solzhenitsyn is sure the United States is no match for Russia at this game, for the Russians, he avows, have murder in their sweet talk and will strike for total victory when they think the moment is ripe. "In our country," says Solzhenitsyn, speaking of his native Russia, "the lie has become not just a moral category but a pillar of the state." Solzhenitsyn remonstrated with the West in the very strongest language for providing the Soviets with the shovels to bury the freedom-loving peoples of the world both within and beyond Russia. The lifetime socialist and former deputy leader of the British Labour Party, Lord George Brown, was so moved by Solzhenitsyn's plea that he immediately defected from the left-leaning Labour Party to veer to the right, becoming a public proponent of preserving democracy through discipline and hard work. Russia's push of atheistic Communism around the globe has been extremely extensive and frighteningly effective, especially in Africa where the whole continent seems again to be up for grabs.

How interested the communists are in world conquest can be seen in the Rockefeller Commission, which reports that, worldwide, communists have currently fully a half-million spies. At the twenty-fifth Congress of the Communist Party in Moscow, the Soviets reaffirmed their open intention to support militantly all communist revolutions throughout the world, wherever they occur. This, despite the fact that they talk out of the other side of their mouth about "detente with 'redoubled energy'" (Leonid Brezhev's statement). The liberal *Toronto Star* in a lead editorial, reviews, continent by continent, the frightening gains of Communism since Nixon, Kissinger, and Brezhnev instituted the current period of "Detente" *(sic)*. The editorialist reckons we're right back "to the bad old Cold War with one important difference: only one side is still waging it with any vigor. Not only the United States but also its allies, including Canada, are using detente to shirk their responsibilities on behalf of democracy. The Soviet Union barely tries to hide the fact that detente is a swindle at the West's expense. It's time the West recognized it as such, and stiffened its foreign policies accordingly." Indicative of the fact that neither the United States nor Canada has had enough desire to "stiffen" their policies consistently was the instance of Daniel Moynihan being withdrawn as the Ambassador to the United Nations for making a statement to the effect that in the United States we castigate the West for colonization, but we hear "not one word on the reality of that European imperial power which had boldly commenced recolonization of the continent of Africa," and, again, Canada's Trudeau went to Castro's Cuba to pour accolades on a communist who even at that moment had his soldiers taking over Angola and who was deliberately using the occasion to announce to the world what he was doing. Just to keep all of us North Americans vigilant, the UPI gives us this warning: "The Soviet Union maintains a permanent nuclear strike force in Cuba capable of wiping out as much as two-thirds of the United States in a nuclear war." Economically, the Soviets are in the best shape they've ever been in. NATO economists note that "the soaring prices of oil and gold have been a windfall for the Soviet Union which has huge supplies of both. The Soviet Union is in the process of becoming one of the leading financial powers." In 1974, the Soviet Union surpassed the United States as the world's leading oil producer.

Certainly the Bible refers to the Soviets and their satellites in Ezekiel 38 and 39. We know from our Lord's explicit reference that Daniel was prophesying specifically about events that would transpire prior to Christ's return. "At the time of the end," envisaged Daniel, speaking from a Jewish geographical perspective, the ruler of "the uttermost part of the north" will sweep down and wage war "like a whirlwind" with "many ships." Russia and her satellites are logically the only power to answer this description, Moscow being almost exactly north of Jerusalem, and the Soviet Union stretching out 6,000 miles in breadth and 3,000 in depth. "Like a whirlwind" may or may not refer to air transports but "many ships" is not an analogy. Russia presently the most powerful navy in the world. *Izvestia* now boldly remonstrates that the "U.S. Navy should abandon the Mediterranean," as more and more Russian ships move down through the Dardanelles. It was recently announced that Russia now has more ships in the Mediterranean than the United States—a very new situation. And with Russia obtaining her first naval and air bases in Southeast Asian waters—in Sri Lanka—she is entrenched in the Indian Ocean. A great British Naval Commander remarked a hundred years ago that the power that could ultimately gain control of the waters of the Indian Ocean would best be situated to conquer the world.

Events move with breathtaking rapidity toward their finality in this arena of activity. Baghdad radio announces that the Soviet Union and Iraq (Syria) have signed a pact "strengthening the Arab hand in the struggle against Israel." NATO goes into special session to consider what to do in the light of the fact that the Prime Minister of Malta, a leftist, ejects NATO forces to make room for the Soviets, who begin a naval installation and the setting up of antiaircraft missiles in the Sudan in which some four hundred to five hundred Russian technicians and twelve to twenty-four SAM-2 missile launchers are said to be involved. The report represents the first indication of a major Soviet buildup in the Sudan. Is it any wonder that *Newsweek*, in an article on "Prophets in Jerusalem," in reference to this, speaks of "the conflict between the Soviet Union and Israel, the emerging battle of Armageddon between the King of the North and the King of the South—the apocalyptic adversaries described in the Book of Daniel"?

In Ezekiel 38 and 39, the details are amazingly explicit. It should be kept in mind that these chapters directly follow Ezekiel's vision of the valley of dry bones, which the prophet interprets in this way: "Thus says the Lord God, 'Behold, I will open your graves and cause you to come up out of your graves, My people, and I will bring you into the land of Israel'" and "I will make them one nation in the land, on the mountains of Israel." Then we read, "Son of man, set thy face toward Gog, of the land of Magog, the prince of Rosh, Meshech, and Tubal, and prophesy against him, and say, Thus says the Lord God, 'Behold, I am against you'" (Ezek. 37:12,22; 38:2,3 NASB).

There is a linguistic clue that this refers to Russia. "Magog" is mentioned in Genesis 10:2 and, according to Josephus, the great first-century Jewish historian, his descendants were the Scythians who migrated to the north, over the Caucasus between the Caspian and Black Seas into what is now Russia. In the evolution of ancient proper nouns into their modern derivatives, it is usual for the consonant sounds generally to remain and the vowels frequently to undergo change. So that "Rosh" is commonly reckoned by lexicographers to be Russia; "Tubal" is thought to be Tobolsk, the Asiatic province of Russia; and "Meshech," Moscow. M. C. Wren's *Ancient Russia* (New York: John Day Company, 1965) makes apposite reading here.

There is evidence again that these chapters refer to Russia in the fact that, as with the Daniel passage, their hordes come from "the uttermost part of the north." The atheistic philosophy that impels them would be another indicator. Ezekiel refers to them as "the heathen." A headline in the editorial section of the *Toronto Star* reads: "Stalin's shadow again darkens the Soviet Union." The article shows that the hard line of militarism and atheism are again being followed. According to the Melbourne *Age*, Stalin executed "at least one in every 20" Jews. Will such treatment go unjudged? Not if the Word of God is true. And in the eighties we read much of a return by the Soviets to Stalinism. Robert Conquest in his book *The Great Terror*, a study of Communism in depth, states, "It is now indisputable that the durability of Soviet totalitarianism is structured on the routinization of terror!" Is it to be wondered that such a country has not published a Bible for public procural since 1957? Is it to be considered out of character that Russia persecutes and humiliates Christians with relentless abuse? As *Fiddler on the Roof* portrays, Russia drives Jews out just because they are Jews, and, according to a Toronto rabbi back from a visit to Moscow, "the noose is tightening" on his people there. Is it possible to say, on the one hand, that God is just and on the other, that He will not bring such a regime to judgment?

The ancient prophet Ezekiel states that this power will resolve to "go up to the land of unwalled villages . . . all of them dwelling without walls, and having neither bars nor gates, to take a spoil, and to take a prey . . . [from] the people that are gathered out of the nations" (Ezek. 38:11,12). This "people" unmistakably refers to restored Israel. "In that day when my people of Israel dwelleth safely . . . thou shalt come from thy place out of the north parts, thou, and many people with thee" (the Soviet Union has, of course, many communist satellites) a "great company and a mighty army: and thou shalt come up against my people of Israel, as a cloud to cover the land; it shall be in the latter days" (vv. 14-16). This is a striking statement, but scarcely more so than the one in the following verse, after the explanation "that the heathen [what could be more heathen than atheistic Communism?] may know me . . . before their eyes. Thus saith the Lord God; Art thou he of whom I have spoken in old time by my servants the prophets of Israel, which prophesied in those days many years?" (v. 17). In short, fulfilled prophecy always vindicates the character and authority of God.

Russian Communism baffles its watchers. Winston Churchill sighed, "I cannot forecast to you the action of Russia. It is a riddle, wrapped in a mystery, inside an enigma." When Russia invaded Czechoslovakia (on the day the nuclear-ban treaty was to have been signed), the liberal *Toronto Star*, Canada's largest newspaper, editorially conceded that for several years it has completely failed in its efforts to forecast the action of Russia. Canada's former Prime Minister, the late Lester Pearson, said, "In my view, communist leaders have not abandoned their ideological desire to establish Communism throughout the world." Lenin said, "Treaties are only for getting breath for a new effort. They exist to be broken as soon as expedient. Peace propaganda is to camouflage war preparations."

So it was hardly unexpected that early in his administration, President Reagan should say that the Soviets have "publicly declared that the only morality they recognize is what will further their cause, meaning they reserve unto themselves the right to commit any crime, to lie, to cheat in order to attain that." He later explained: "They don't subscribe to our idea of morality. They don't believe in a God or a religion, and the only morality they recognize, therefore, is what will advance the world of socialism."

The United States Defense Department's research director, Malcolm Currie, reckons that "from all indications, the future Soviet strategy will be world dominance, with technology as one of the key drivers." Not only are the Russians out-producing the Americans in, say, tank production "four to one, it is by no means clear that the Soviet Union regards nuclear war as unthinkable. There is a strong evidence to the contrary."

President Eisenhower had no illusions about the Russian intent. It seemed to him "incredible that such poison be swallowed, but people who have seen so much political wickedness, cold blood, betrayal and godless depravity in government find it harder to believe our peaceful intent than the clever lies Communism is spreading every, every day." Daniel Moynihan writes in the *Harvard* magazine that the Soviets are currently winning their ideological warfare with the United States by "using guilt as a weapon against America, to retard U.S. responses to continuing Communist aggression" worldwide. Such a clever contrivance in the use of "guilt" must be political history's most heinous hypocrisy.

U.S. News and World Report reveals that the Soviet

bloc's military edge over the combined forces of the West is 2-1 in military aircraft, 2-1 in armed manpower, and 3-1 both in armor and in submarines. A United States naval expert stuns the militarists of the world by stating that the military might of the Russian Navy is eight years ahead of that of the Americans. Rabbi Ruben Slonim, in his television interviews, has given a penetrating analysis of how the Russians are pouring more money into the Arab world than into all their other foreign schemes combined, in an effort to obtain free movement from the Mediterranean to the Indian Ocean and to procure the oil and minerals they need. Rabbi Rosenburg, a columnist, states rightly that "the real aggressor in the Middle East is not the Arabs, but the Russians." This has been repeatedly affirmed by Golda Meir and Menachin Begin. The mineral reserves in the Dead Sea area are astronomical, having an estimated value of $1,270,000,000,000, which is the GNP (gross national product) of the whole American nation for nearly a year. The potash alone would fertilize all agricultural lands of the world for several centuries. The most recent boon in the Dead Sea area is an oil-and-gas find—possibly a huge one. So Russia is not unmotivated in her designs on Israel.

It is scarcely to be wondered at that Russia does not intend to let a tiny country like Israel stand in its way. "Israel is the only thing that stands between Russian and a Communist takeover of the Middle East," comments the *Miami Herald*. Moshe Dayan of Israel said, during the Six-Day War in 1967: "Israel is now at war with Russia." These chapters in Ezekiel, which any careful historian knows have had no fulfillment in the past, indicate that Israel's intuitive apprehensions are not without justification. Milovan Djilas, of Yugoslavia reckons that the Russian "party bureaucracy built under Stalin has not changed much structurally since his death. Rather, it has fallen into contradictions and troubles that the bureaucrats cannot solve except by two means: one is to stifle democratic trends within the society; the other is to extend Soviet power outside Russia's borders." Djilas is sure the latter course will be pursued. He is right.

What follows does not make pleasant reading. These invaders from the "uttermost part of the north" sweep down through what must be modern Syria "upon the mountains of Israel." It's important to note here, as *Time* points out, that Syria is a satellite of the Soviets. In 1981 it has been accepted into membership in the Warsaw Pact. It is governed by the Baath Party, which is Marxist both in origin and current commitment. The Russians have armed Syria to the hilt since 1957. They currently have some 3,000 Russian advisers at every level in Syria today but most intensively in the military. So it is no wonder that the route the Soviets take will be through Syria. The Prime Minister of Israel reckons, as reported in *Time*, that the most belligerent of Israel's Arab adversaries are the Syrians, who have been keeping, and will continue to keep, the Arab/Israeli conflict at a brink-of-war pitch at all times. When the war was raging in Lebanon, the AP was diligent to report that the Syrians acted only in concert with their Soviet backers.

Thus, it will be in the region of Syria that God's intervention takes place. This intervention will clearly "vindicate" His existence and bring judgment on the northern invaders. It will have a revolutionizing effect on Israel to turn them to the God of their fathers. The Lord says, "I will plead against him with pestilence and with blood; and I will rain upon him, and upon his bands, and upon the many people that are with him, an overflowing rain and great hailstones, fire, and brimstone" (Ezek. 38:22). Is this the ancient expression of bacteriological and thermonuclear destruction? I do not know: "hailstones, fire, and brimstone" rained down from above. In any event, we read of God's judgment in His Word: "I will turn thee back and leave but the sixth part of thee . . . and seven months shall the house of Israel be burying of them, that they may cleanse the land" (Ezek. 39:2, 12).

Working in alliance with Russia will be Persia (Iran), Libya and Ethiopia (Ezekiel 38:5). It is almost uncanny the way these three nations have fallen into the Soviet sphere along with Syria in the last twenty years. In President

Reagan's first press conference they were referred to as "surrogates" of the Soviets. And it is a truism. You can hardly pick up a *New York Times* or a *Time* without them being linked together as allies of the Russians (Gog the land of Magog, Meshech and Tubal: Ezekiel 38:2), East Germany (Gomer: Ezekiel 38:6), and various other Soviet satellites.

I tend to the opinion that this war will take place shortly after the church, as the Body of Christ, has been raptured to heaven. With such a large percentage of North American saints gone—including leaders—there will be chaos on this continent, and it is my view that the Soviets will march on Israel and meanwhile, may well wipe out much of our beloved American and Canadian peoples. And the destruction of five-sixths of the Soviet military could be the American retaliation, shooting their last nuclear military bolt—as it were. In this horrible holocaustic exchange, one-third of the population of the world will be exterminated, the awful solemnity of this position being that so many victims may well be North Americans who knowingly refuse Christ today. Thus, both superpowers would largely be removed to make room for the Antichrist to take his cakewalk through the earth.

Horrible as this sounds, it is in no way out of line with the warnings of scientists throughout the world. Scriptural prophecy and scientific predictions are terrifyingly coincidental. Only sentimental dreamers ignore the hard facts. One generation ago much of this would have seemed inconceivable. Today no one but a human ostrich denies the stark reality of events racing toward the precipice.

18

THE CHRISTOLOGICAL SIGNS

The prime mover in the events that will march man into World War III (which I am here using as a description of Armageddon) will be the Antichrist. People's readiness today to go gung ho after an Antichrist could be seen in their going to see the Rome-based film *The Antichrist*. Then Americans went for the *The Omen* as the film of the year as they had earlier gone for the *Exorcist* and now for *Damien* and its 1981 sequel. *Time* states that *"The Omen* presents . . . a prophecy about the return of the Prince of Darkness, taken from Revelations to fit certain events of our time—the creation of Israel and the Common Market . . .—then argues persuasively that if satan were to return in disguise," a certain terrifying world situation would prevail. The author of the article wonders darkly if there really might be "faith in these secular times to believe in a reincarnated devil," that, is, the Antichrist. However much attention is being given in the secular world to the Antichrist, it is a certainty that a great deal of attention is given to him in Scripture, where he is depicted, not as a fictional figmentation of the imagination but as a factual reality—a terrible personification of evil who will work more wholesale havoc than any other human being in the history of the world. The apostle John, who makes several references to him, states in his first mention that in "the last hour [of the current age] . . . antichrist is coming" (1 John 2:18). Jesus told His disciples that previous to His coming to earth to judge the nations and set up His kingdom, men would "see standing in the holy place 'the abomination that causes desolation,' spoken of through the prophet Daniel—let the reader understand" (Matt. 24:15).

So we turn to Daniel's description. Here we discover that the Antichrist is a man who arrogates to himself power—wicked, sinister, wonder-working power—and he does just as Jesus said he would do. Halfway through his reign he enters into the temple of God (by that time restored) and desecrates the altar, thereby breaking the covenant he had made with Israel to maintain their peaceful existence.

His diabolical dictatorship is realized; his tyranny of terror becomes a reality. He shows himself to have been the most monstrous wolf in sheep's clothing in history as he sets out to conquer the world. The last half of his dominance Daniel sets at three and a half years, meaning that he will be on the scene for approximately seven years after his manifestation. "In the midst" of his reign, we read, "he shall cause the sacrifice and the oblation to cease, and for the overspreading of abominations he shall make it desolate, even until the consummation [the return of Jesus Christ to the earth], "and that determined shall be poured upon the desolate" (Dan. 9:27). "And from the time that the daily sacrifice shall be taken away, and the abomination that maketh desolate set up, there shall be a thousand two hundred and ninety days" (Dan. 12:11). The Book of Revelation gives the time as forty-two months. The Antichrist will not so much deny the existence of God, which Communism does, as deny His authority. "Antichrist," wrote the apostle John, "denies the Father and the Son" for "no one who denies the Son has the Father" (1 John 2:22, 23 KJV).

He "shall do according to his will; and he shall exalt

himself, and magnify himself above every god," foretold Daniel, "and shall speak marvelous things against the God of gods, and shall prosper till the indignation to be accomplished: for that that is determined shall be done. Neither shall he regard the God of his fathers, nor the desire of women, nor regard any god: for he shall magnify himself above all. But in his estate shall he honour the God of forces: and a god whom his fathers knew not shall he honour with gold, and silver, and with precious stones, and pleasant things" (Dan. 11:36-38 KJV).

We see on our television sets superbowls, superboy, superlight, supermouse, superman, and superstars and in *Time* a cover feature on "Stars and Anti-stars." While there is obviously nothing intrinsically wrong with these usages, they presage a preconditioning for the acceptance of the Antichrist when he comes. Everywhere there is a craving for authority and order. During the post–World War II era, more than half of the world's governments have been overthrown by coup d'etat. *Time* currently points to the instability of governments in Western Europe. In the last few years there has been a change of leadership in all ten nations of the European Common Market. For a "superman" to move into that kind of flux and galvanize a supra-autocracy is no longer at all unthinkable. Reasons *Time:* "Being a leader in any country is no great fun these days. All industrial societies face intractable problems that the leadership is not capable of coping with." *Time* recently stated, "The real aim of the Market (ECC) is, of course, to become one single country." The United Nations Secretary-General has declared, "I do not wish to seem overdramatic, but I can only conclude from the information that is available to me as Secretary-General that the members of the United Nations have perhaps ten years left in which to subordinate their ancient quarrels and launch a global partnership to curb the arms race, to improve the human environment, to defuse the population explosion, and to supply the required momentum to world development efforts." The alternative, is a situation "beyond our capacity to control."

Shortly before his death, Bertrand Russell said that we must very soon have world government or universal annihilation. He was right. Dr. Henri Spaak, the world-famous statesman from Belgium, has expressed how crucially man needs a superstatesman. "The truth is that the method of international committees has failed," he reasons, and "the highest order of experience" indicates that only a world ruler can control the world. "Let him come, and let him come quickly" and "galvanize all governments" and "let him vanquish" anarchy from the earth. Roy Fuller, a poetry professor at Oxford, argues eloquently how close Europe and America are to a dictatorship. With the late Walter Lippmann's comment that the world is apparently ungoverned and ungovernable, it was not surprising to see an editorial predicting that one day even the Americans may well have to resort to a military dictatorship. Both the Prime Ministers Margaret Thatcher of Britain and Pierre Trudeau of Canada warn their countrymen of beckoning dictatorship. Canada's best-known television commentator, Pierre Berton, laments that all the countries of South America, with the exception of Uruguay, have resorted to militarists as their heads of government as the only way to get law and order. And the trend is sweeping the world. In the so-called "free world," says Berton, "politics has become a hunt for a messiah," quoting as a case in point an American governor who said that as he looked at the spectrum of political candidates running for the presidency, frankly, "I am looking for a messiah, and no one measures up." The late Cambridge historian Arnold Toynbee reckoned that man in his present panic is "ripe for the deifying of any new Caesar who might succeed in giving the world unity and peace."

Jeane Dixon, the world-famous Catholic prognosticator, has with interesting accuracy forecast many happenings over the last few years, such as the time and place of the assassinations of both of the Kennedys. "Believing in Jeane Dixon," remarks a national weekly, "has become something of a religion in this country." In the book *A Gift of Prophecy* she claims that the strongest impression by far that she has ever had was the one she received on February 4, 1962, the day on which, she is convinced, a coming world ruler was born. The biblical Christian does not, as a matter of principle, put stock in human predictions, but some are difficult to ignore.

In four of the five New Testament books the apostle John wrote, he refers to the coming Antichrist. In two of his three epistles he uses the term "antichrist" and in the Revelation, where he traces the rise, reign of terror, and demise of the Antichrist in considerable detail, he calls him the "Beast." Paul describes him as the "man of sin"; NIV, "man of lawlessness." History began with the sin of man and closes with the "man of sin." As John described how he had taught a good deal about the coming Antichrist ("as ye have heard"), so Paul parenthesizes his description of this coming vile dictator with the reminder to the Thessalonians that when he was with them, he had treated this theme in depth: "You cannot but remember that I told you this while I was still with you" (2 Thess. 2:5 NEB). So apparently a great deal was said about Antichrist in apostolic preaching.

Before we mention a limited number of salient features of the rule of the coming Antichrist, let us explore Paul's treatment of this "man of lawlessness" in 2 Thessalonians 2. He is to "be revealed in human form, the man doomed to perdition. He is the Enemy. He rises in his pride against every god, so called, every object of men's worship, and even takes his seat in the temple of God claiming to be a god himself." Paul further explains, "You must now be aware of the restraining hand which ensures that he shall be revealed only at the proper time. For already the secret power of wickedness is at work, secret only for the present until the Restrainer disappears from the scene. And then he will be revealed, that wicked man [the 'man of lawlessness'] whom the Lord Jesus will destroy with the breath of his mouth, and annihilate by the radiance of his coming. But the coming of that wicked man is the work of Satan. It will be attended by all the powerful signs and miracles of the Lie, and all the deception that sinfulness can impose on those doomed to destruction" (2 Thess. 2:3, 4, 6-10 NEB). The *New Catholic Encyclopedia* (1966) states, "Catholic theologians have been nearly unanimous in maintaining that the anti-Christ will be an individual person. . . . The anti-Christ is preserved, for the 'last times,' his tyranny to 'extend' to the second coming of Jesus Christ, who will vanquish and obliterate him, and set up His kingdom on earth."

Who is the Antichrist? As the *New Catholic Encyclopedia* points out, all through church history zealous prophets have audaciously identified certain characters or movements as "the Antichrist," only to fall thereby into theological discredit. The same source further indicates, as the apostle Paul clearly states, that while precursors of the Antichrist may well harbinger his coming (a point John made by calling these "many antichrists"), the real Antichrist will not be known until "someone or something" who (or which) restrains the forces of evil in general and the Antichrist in particular, is removed. This is, of course, based on the fact that Paul says clearly that the Antichrist will not be revealed until "the Restrainer disappears from the scene." Theologians throughout church history have been divided as to whether the Restrainer is the church or the Holy Spirit. I would tend toward the latter view but, either way, the meaning is not altered. On the Day of Pentecost, the Holy Spirit was given in a special way, as Jesus had repeatedly promised He would be, to call out and control the church of Jesus Christ, and with the "gathering together unto Him" (Christ), the description of the rapture of the church with which Paul opens this chapter, the special gift of the Holy Spirit will be withdrawn.

Thus, with all true Christians in heaven with Christ —whether they be Calvinist or Armenian, Protestant or Catholic, of the apostolic or atomic age—on earth, there will be no "Restrainer." Then, and then only, will be "the proper time" for the Antichrist to be revealed. It is as wrong, from both scriptural and practical points of view, to try to identify the Antichrist as it is to name a date for the return of

Christ. Both errors have recurringly brought the preaching of biblical prophecy into needless and harmful disrepute, and this not only in the twentieth century, but all through church history.

What will be the empire of the Antichrist? Most encyclopedias, whether secular, Protestant, or Catholic, basing their view on Daniel 2 and 7 and Revelation 13 and 17, indicate that generally it will initially coincide with the ancient Roman Empire. (This view was given worldwide publicity through its expression in *The Omen*.) This empire will constitute a bloc of ten Western nations. According to the apostle John, when the Antichrist is on the ascendancy, he will incorporate the power of ten rulers into his own iron hand "to share with the beast the exercise of royal authority; for they have but a single purpose among them and will confer their power and authority upon the beast" (Rev. 17:13, NEB). In regard to chronological order, it seems that the war in which the Soviets are destroyed as they try to descend into Israel will take place early in the "Great Tribulation." About then, the Antichrist will be killed, descend into perdition, and arise from the dead. Consolidating his hold in Jerusalem, he will send out his forces to conquer the whole world, over which he will hold an iron hand, though his rule will be comparatively short-lived. That the world is ominously awaiting such a dictator can be seen in the communique from the Club of Rome, which warns "Crisis leads to war and war today means nuclear conflagration, which in turn spells collective suicide . . . only a global plan . . . can avert universal catastrophe."

In his BBC telecasts, the late Canadian Prime Minister Lester Pearson urged a unifying and solidifying of the states of Western Europe, a move that first found pragmatic expression in General George C. Marshall's now-historic address at Harvard on June 5, 1947. A year or two ago, it looked as if Western Europe, as drawn together through NATO, was disintegrating again. Now with the Russian rape of Afghanistan, and the recrudescence of Stalinism, there is a new craving for solidarity in Europe and a vacuum for leadership into which a dictator could well step and usurp command. Former Prime Minister of Britain Edward Heath had been a passionate proponent of British entry into the European Common Market for a decade before leading Britain into it. *Time* said that when the ECC expanded from six to ten countries, Europe was thus achieving her "greatest unity since the beginning of the breakup of Charlemagne's Empire in 814." In 1976, with the death of Franco, Spain made overtures that would expand the ECC "nine" into "ten." Notes *Newsweek:* "Spain wants to join both the Common Market and the North Atlantic Treaty Organization."

When the Antichrist takes over, he will unify the currency, a move that De Gaulle in his closing days of power promoted. The European Common Market, with its imposing headquarters in Brussels, has already taken strides in this direction. Traditionalist Britain and Ireland, upon entering the ECC, both moved to join the trend by converting to the decimal system. *Time* notes, "One month after the latest international monetary crisis, cabinet officers, legislators and bankers on both sides of the Atlantic are intensely debating a lengthening list of ideas" for developing a "global financial system." For many decades Bible scholars have been predicting this.

"In his estate shall he honour the God of forces" (Dan. 11:38). The Antichrist will be a militarist. In this he will be like Mao Tse-tung, one of whose sayings was that nothing is useful that does not come out of the barrel of a cannon. The fact that he will perform great and miraculous signs, even causing "fire to come down from heaven to earth in full view of men" (Rev. 13:13), may or may not refer to thermonuclear devices. But his social structuring strikingly resembles the predictions of moderns. The Hollywood film *The Omen* has striking parallels to the way the Antichrist will operate. A book like George Orwell's *1984* finds ominous parallels in Revelation: Antichrist "caused everyone, great and small, rich and poor, slave and free, to be branded with a mark on his right hand or forehead, and no one was allowed to buy or sell unless he bore this beast's mark, either name or number" (Rev. 13:17 NEB). Social Security numbers demonstrate the viability of this. In fact, every newborn baby in the Netherlands today is given a number. There is now a process whereby a number can be imprinted invisibly on your hand or forehead by an electronic device and can be read at a glance with an instrument. Disney World in Florida is already using such a process. Increasingly, numbers are replacing names in our world, and while machines are acting more and more like men, men are acting more and more like machines.

Will moderns actually "worship the image of the beast"? On the Dick Cavett Show" in 1981, Cavett alluded to a head of state, he had on his program who "actually thought he was god!" UPI carried an article in January 1981 on the view of the Britain neurologist Dr. Frank Elliot, who had observed Joseph R. Stalin first-hand and had also studied Hitler. Elliot is of the opinion that many humans, once they're in power, are not only corupted, but go mad and become megalomaniacs. They lose their capacity for emotion and can lie, steal, blame others, and become cruel and ruthless, with a strange inability to feel guilt or shame. So to "worship the image of the Beast." We would have scorned this possibility until Hitler elicited a semblance of this kind of thing. Another example is the Beatles, whose records, following the shooting of John Lennon are again topping the charts. Derek Taylor, their press agent, observed the reaction they evoked when they were on tour in the sixties: "It's absolutely rude, profane, vulgar; taken over the world, they are completely antichrist. Sick people rushed up. It was as if some saviour had arrived. The only thing left for the Beatles to do is to go on a healing tour. I'm antichrist, but these boys even shock me." Under the byline "Growing Antichrist Movement in This Country," the *Minneapolis Tribune* argues that with Christianity effectively abolished from the schools, there is evidence everywhere that it now seems necessary "to infiltrate our schools with the occult, to the point of teaching it in classes and also bringing in transcendental meditation, which is nothing more than the Hindu religion."

In Matthew 24, Jesus intimates that when the Antichrist desecrates the temple of God (with three and a half years of his tenure left, as Daniel and the apostle John both indicate), he will bring such persecution upon believers that it will be a period that Jesus called the "Great Tribulation" (Matt. 24:21 KJV): a time "unequaled from the beginning of the world until now and never to be equaled again." Jesus was obviously referring personally to the Antichrist when He said people would "see standing in the holy place 'the abomination that causes desolation,' spoken of through the prophet Daniel—let the reader understand" (Matt. 24:21,15).

Looking for loopholes for unbelief and prodigal living, as man is always prone to do, many at this point ask: Is it not possible for me to reject Jesus Christ as Savior and Lord here and now, as I will have opportunity to repent and then to be saved during that period of "great tribulation" to which Jesus referred, after the rapture of the church to heaven? I do not believe so. For the gospel preached during those terrible times will be to those who have never heard. Those who have heard and rejected Christ as Savior and Lord will fall into the category of Paul's description in 2 Thessalonians 2: "The coming of the lawless one by the activity of Satan will be with all power and with pretended signs and wonders, and with all wicked deception for those who are to perish, because they refused to love the truth and so be saved. Therefore God sends upon them a strong delusion, to make them believe what is false, so that all may be condemned who did not believe the truth but had pleasure in unrighteousness" (vv. 9-11 RSV). Since this is the age of the Holy Spirit, the unpardonable sin is being committed by those who ignore the Spirit's call to Christ. When Jesus Christ comes to receive His church as we rise "to meet the Lord in the air," the present invitation of the Holy Spirit will be withdrawn.

When and where will the Battle of Armageddon be

fought? The actual time is indicated by the prophet Daniel, by John in the Revelation, and by our Lord, as being just prior to the second coming of Jesus Christ to this earth. It will be, as I understand it, some time after Christ's coming to meet and receive His church in the air, immediately prior to the revelation of Jesus Christ. It will be fought on the plain of Megiddo (also referred to as Armageddon and the Valley of Jehoshaphat), the fourteen-by-twenty-mile tract of land that Napoleon allegedly appraised as the most ideal place on earth for a military battle.

"Armageddon," according to the *New Catholic Encyclopedia*, will be the place where the Antichrist will summon the kings of the earth for the final battle of mankind. The Southern, Northern, and Eastern blocs of nations will all converge to engage the Antichrist and his forces. Accounts in Daniel, Zechariah, 2 Thessalonians, and Revelation tell of blocs of nations coming from the South. In Addis Ababa, Ethiopia, in 1963 such a bloc of potential nations was formed: the Organization of African Unity. If China leads the forces from the East, they are already announcing that they have a milita of 200 million, ready to march. "Let China sleep," Napoleon advocated, "for when China awakes, let the nations tremble." If Babylon is restored literally, as I currently think is highly possible under the hegemonical leadership of perhaps a Hussein, it will already have been destroyed (see Revelation 18). And then, of course, the bloc from the North will be what remains of the Soviets and the Arab Confederation.

The biblical accounts of Armageddon are many, and they are surely among the most dramatic in all literature. "The spirits of devils, working miracles, which go forth unto the kings of the earth and of the whole world, to gather them to the battle of that great day of God Almighty," writes John in the Revelation of Jesus Christ, "and he gathered them together into a place called in the Hebrew tongue Armageddon" (Rev. 16:14, 16, KJV).

Joel the prophet foresaw all the heathen Gentile nations resolving to "prepare war, stir up the mighty men. Let all the men of war draw near, let them come up. Beat your plowshares into swords, and your pruninghooks into spears . . . and come up to the valley of Jehoshaphat" (Joel 3:9, 10, RSV). Here Armageddon will be fought. General Douglas MacArthur reckoned, "We have had our last chance. The Battle of Armageddon comes next!"

I was in London the week after the June 1967 war between Israel and the Arabs. The *Times* carried a remarkable lead editorial on how close we may be to Armageddon, identifying the place, time, and combatants of such a war. Mr. Eisenhower replied to Lord Montgomery in perhaps their last communication that unless peace can be negotiated, then it is Armageddon. *Armageddon* is the title of a best seller. When *Time* is casting about for a word to describe a bloody university skirmish, it describes it as "the Armageddon of the Computer Age." "Will tonight's matchup be a Stanley Cup hockey game or a preview of Armageddon?" asks a CBC television commentator in a metaphor all fans understand well!

The Antichrist will gain his mandate, not as a warmonger, but as a promiser of peace. Many people, from Franklin D. Roosevelt to Twiggy, have said, "I hate war!" General Sherman said, "War is hell!" Man will end up at his technocratic best and his moral worst. Jesus said of Armageddon, "If those days had not been cut short, no one would survive" (Matt. 24:22). The Pope in New York quotes President Kennedy: "Mankind must put an end to war, or war will put an end to mankind." Great men agree that man is drifting toward the edge of the precipice.

Will Armageddon be the end of human life? No. As Arnold Toynbee said not long before his death in 1975: "I believe the human race will not commit suicide—it will stop just short of that." Actually man would exterminate himself at Armageddon except for the fact that just when it appears that he will annihilate himself, Jesus, the real Christ, will come—and just in time. One of the earliest prophecies in history, as recorded by the apostle Jude, is that of Enoch, the seventh from Adam, who foresaw this climax of history: "See, the Lord is coming with thousands upon thousands of his holy ones to judge everyone, and to convict all the ungodly of all their ungodly acts they have done in their ungodly way, and of all the harsh words ungodly sinners have spoken against him" (Jude 14, 15). Jesus foresaw His second advent to earth and apprised His disciples who had gathered with Him on the Mount of Olives: "At that time they will see the Son of Man coming in a cloud with power and great glory" (Luke 21:27). For, as Zechariah predicted, "the day of the Lord is coming," when He shall "gather all the nations against Jerusalem . . . on the east, and the Mount of Olives shall be split in two from east to west by a very wide valley; so that one half of the Mount shall withdraw northward and the other half southward" (Zech. 14:2, 4), something that seismologists have known for years is highly probable. In Revelation 16, it is called "a violent earthquake, like none before it in human history, so violent it was (Rev. 16:18 NEB).

In fact, as Dr. Charles Taylor has pointed out in 1981, it will open up a waterway from the Mediterranean to the Dead Sea and drain southward through the Gulf of Aqaba into the Red Sea. Ezekiel prophecies of those millennial waters.

And so Jesus Christ the Lord will come on His white horse. At the time of President Reagan's inauguration in 1981, Johnny Carson asked: "Is President Reagan the Man on the White Horse, or the man in the White House? President Reagan is the man in the White House. Jesus Christ is the Man on the White Horse. Paul wrote that Jesus will consume the Antichrist with the brightness of His coming. Both for magnificence and glorious truth, there is no more dramatic description in all literature than the following preview of the moment when our Lord returns to earth as foreseen by John. In Revelation 19 he "saw heaven standing open and there before me was a white horse, whose rider is called Faithful and True. With justice He judges and makes war. His eyes are like blazing fire and on his head are many crowns. He has a name written on him that no one but he himself knows. He is dressed in a robe dipped in blood, and his name is the Word of God. The armies of heaven were following him, riding on white horses and dressed in fine linen, white and clean. Out of his mouth comes a sharp sword with which to strike down the nations. He will rule them with a rod of iron . . . On his robe and on his thigh he has this name written: KING OF KINGS AND LORD OF LORDS. . . . Then I saw the beast and the kings of the earth and their armies gathered together to make war against the rider on the horse and his army. But the beast was captured, and with him the false prophet who had performed the miraculous signs on his behalf. With these signs he had deluded those who had received the mark of the beast and worshiped his image. The two of them were thrown alive into the fiery lake of burning sulfur" (Rev. 19:11-14, 16, 19-21). In the fourth century, Jerome the church father forecast, "No one shall be able to assist the antichrist as the Lord vents His fury upon them. Antichrist is going to perish in that spot from which our Lord ascended to heaven."

As the *New Catholic Encyclopedia* points out, the result of Christ's triumph over Antichrist and the forces of evil will be the advent of the millennium, a thousand-year reign of Jesus Christ and His saints of all the ages over an earth that will know unprecedented prosperity and peace. John foresaw in the Revelation, as Armageddon concludes with the glorious triumph of our Lord, how God bound Satan "for a thousand years . . . that he might seduce the nations no more till the thousand years were over." Furthermore, he "saw thrones, and upon them sat those to whom judgement was committed. I could see the souls of those who had been beheaded for the sake of God's word and their testimony to Jesus, those who had not worshipped the beast and its image or received its mark on forehead or hand. These came to life again and reigned with Christ for a thousand years, though the rest of the dead did not come to life until the thousand years were over." These are "happy indeed," exults John, for "they shall be priests of God and of

Christ, and shall reign with him for the thousand years" (Rev. 20:2-6, NEB). "Everything we know," said Nobel prize-winning chemist Willard Libby, "implies that the opportunities for future development are unbounded for a rational society operating without war." This, I suggest, will be realized during the earthly reign of our Lord.

From time immemorial, man has longed for a combination on this earth of law and order, peace and prosperity, freedom and fulfillment, health and happiness, godliness and longevity. It will happen when Christ comes again to this earth to set up His kingdom. The pope was right when he told the visiting rock group delegation, "It is not in my power to abolish war." Only Jesus Christ can do that. Two New York lawyers, Grenville Clark and Louis Sohn, wrote their classic, *World Peace Through World Law*, 3rd ed., rev., enl. (Cambridge: Harvard University Press, 1966). The question is: Who is to effect the "Law"? The answer is that peace and law can only happen when Christ comes again.

"In the last days," noted the ancient prophet Micah in a passage a United States president alludes to in his inauguration address, "it shall come to pass, that the mountain of the house of the Lord shall be established in the top of the mountains, and it shall be exalted above the hills; and people shall flow unto it. And many nations shall come and say, Come, and let us go up to the mountain of the Lord, and to the house of the God of Jacob; and he will teach us of his ways, and we will walk in his paths: for the law shall go forth of Zion, and the word of the Lord from Jerusalem. And he shall judge among many people, and rebuke strong nations . . . and they shall beat their swords into plowshares, and their spears into pruninghooks: nation shall not lift up sword against nation, neither shall they learn war any more" (Micah 4:1-4 KJV). *Time* tells us that while the number of the world's doctor's, teachers, and engineers is currently increasing only slowly, that of army officers is rising dramatically. The return of Christ will immediately reverse this. Indeed, there will be no need for the military at all, for Christ Himself will reign. Gone will be the current annual budget of 600 billion dollars for armaments. Military uniforms will be collectors' items. Then and then only will be fulfilled that glorious vision of the ancient Isaiah, which no peace demonstration or human negotiations can effect: "The government will be on his [Jesus Christ's] shoulders. And he will be named Wonderful Counselor, Mighty God, Everlasting Father, Prince of Peace. Of the extension of his government and peace there will be no end" (Isa. 9:6,7). And all of the world will commune in symphony:

> Our Father who art in heaven,
>   hallowed be Thy name.
> Thy kingdom come, Thy will be done
>   on earth as it is in heaven.
> Give us this day our daily bread.
> And forgive us our debts, as we forgive
>   our debtors.
> And lead us not into temptation, but deliver us
>   from evil.
> For Thine is the kingdom, and the power, and the
>   glory, for ever. Amen.

The Bible declares that there is hope for eternal life and that that hope is in Christ. Paul wrote to Titus of "the hope of eternal life, which God, who does not lie, promised before the beginning of time" (Titus 1:2). Pope John Paul II told a gathering of car drivers and mechanics in Rome in 1981 that really "we're all on the high road headed for eternity." Dr. Donn Moomaw in his prayer at the inauguration of President Ronald Reagan, invoked God to keep reminding us to keep measuring "always the shortness of time and the length of eternity."

The believer in Christ has an eternity with the Lord—"Free at Last"—to which to look forward. Therefore every believer's ultimate is not a downer but an upper! Christ is coming down so that we may go up! So we should not dig ourselves into a hole. We should stand on the hill of hope, scanning the horizon, not for a nuclear holocaust, but for the host of heaven who will transport us to the skies. Jesus Christ is preparing to come and, in the greatest airlift of all time, will take His church to heaven. Except for that, Paul wrote, the Christian would be, of all men, most miserable; but with such an expectation we are "joyful in hope" (Rom. 12:12).

Those theologians who don't believe in Christ's coming again capitulate to despair. In the sixties, Thomas J. J. Altizer, Professor of Bible and Religion at Emory University, introduced his "God is dead" theory. More recently he had to write somberly of the abject "hopelessness in today's world."

The Bible is the only reliable guide to the future. A syndicated newspaper cartoon reads, "A man with one watch knows the time—a man with two is never sure." For a sure guide to what time it is on God's clock, turn to the Scriptures and settle on them as the sole authoritative timetable of man's future. Astrologers, fortune tellers, or even scientific futurists are all in a state of inane confusion when it comes to the world of tomorrow. Jesus said, "Watch." Watch what? The Word of God! Where do we go for such hope? To the Scriptures!

An overview of the events involved in the coming again of Jesus Christ and the end of the age occupies some 1,845 Scripture verses. Focusing on this theme, the biblical assurance of the Lord's coming again is *prophesied in the Old Testament*. In fact, long before Moses wrote Genesis, "Enoch, the seventh from Adam, prophesied . . ., 'See, the Lord is coming . . .'" (Jude 14). Undoubtedly, it was of the Lord's return that Jacob spoke in his famous last words to his sons: "The scepter [which means 'He to whom it belongs'] shall not depart from Judah until Shiloh comes, whom all people shall obey" (Gen. 49:10 LB). Numerous times in the Old Testament, we read of "the last days," "the latter times," and that "the day of the Lord is coming" (e.g., Joel 2:1). Malachi, in the penultimate verse of the Old Testament, prophesies of "the great and dreadful day of the Lord" (Mal. 4:5)—for the saved, "great"; for the lost, "dreadful."

The Lord's second coming is surely to be seen in the Old Testament, but is only clear when we turn to the New Testament. *The promises in the New Testament* concerning His return are unmistakably plain. Jesus assured His disciples: "I will not leave you as orphans; I will come to you." So "do not let your hearts be troubled. Trust in God; trust also in Me. There are many rooms in my Father's house; otherwise, I would have told you. I am going there to prepare a place for you. And if I go and prepare a place for you, I will come back and take you to be with me that you also may be where I am" (John 14:1-3, 18). On many other occasions, Jesus reassured His followers that though He would go away, He would return to the planet earth to get His own so that they would be at home with Him forever.

After He was crucified and risen and forty days had passed, and just before He ascended from the view of five hundred of His disciples who saw Him off, Jesus saw to it that they were reassured of His return. They were still "looking intently up into the sky as He was going, when suddenly two men dressed in white stood beside them. 'Men of Galilee,' they said, 'why do you stand here looking into the sky? This same Jesus, who has been taken from you into heaven, will come back in the same way you have seen him go into heaven'" (Acts 1:10, 11).

Such was this final impression of the incarnate Son of God on His apostles that every one of them who wrote Epistles used the assurance of Christ's imminent coming again to exhort Christians, as Martin Luther put it, to live as though Christ died yesterday, rose again today, and were coming to receive and reward His own tomorrow. Looking upward meant looking inward for purification, looking outward in compassion, and looking onward with expectation that all will be well. So we turn to the Epistles and read John's counsel: "Dear friends, now we are children of God, and what we will be has not yet been made known. But we know that when he appears, we shall be like him, for we shall see him as he is. Everyone who has this hope in him purifies himself, just as he is pure" (1 John 3:2, 3). Peter also enjoined holy living: Since "the day of the Lord will come like a thief . . . what kind of people ought you to be? You ought to live holy and godly lives, as you look forward to the day of God and speed its coming" (2 Peter 3:10-12). James urged us to "stand firm, because the Lord's coming is near" (James 5:8). Since "the Lord is coming," admonished Jude, "you, dear friends, build yourselves up in your most holy faith and pray in the Holy Spirit. Keep yourselves in God's love as you wait for the mercy of our Lord Jesus Christ to bring you to eternal life" (Jude 14, 20, 21). Paul, in the passage that was Winston Churchill's favorite, exulted, "Listen, I tell you a mystery: We shall not all sleep, but we shall all be changed—in a flash, in the twinkling of an eye, at the last trumpet. For the trumpet will sound, the dead will be raised imperishable, and we shall be changed. For the perishable must clothe itself with the imperishable, and the mortal with immortality. . . . Therefore, my dear brothers, stand firm. Let nothing move you. Always give yourselves fully to the work of the Lord, because you know that your labor in the Lord is not in vain" (1 Cor. 15:51-53, 58). "In a very little while, he who is coming will come and will not be late"; therefore, exhorted the writer to the Hebrews, "you need to persevere so that when you have done the will of God, you will receive what he has promised" (Heb. 10:36, 37). Finally, as the capstone of New Testament eschatological hope and as His last written message to the church, Jesus said, "Yes, I am coming soon." John the aged, who was sinking into life's sunset and looking forward to sunrise, exclaimed in response: "Amen. Come, Lord Jesus" (Rev. 22:20).

There is one thing, however, that is more important than the preaching of the second coming of Christ. It is the preaching of the Christ of the second coming. The two are inseparable, of course. From ancient times, the proclamation of the former has turned millions of people to seek the latter. Gwen Beck, a schoolteacher, told me in Cody, Wyoming, where I was holding a crusade that four years earlier her life was unbroken confusion. A suspecting sister on the East Coast sent her a copy of *Re-Entry*—my earlier book on the second coming of Christ. When Gwen read it, the warning of Jesus that we are to "be ready" for the coming again of Christ especially touched her. Gwen said, "I simply was not a Christian. This led me to confess on my knees that I was a sinner and I asked Christ to come into my life and to be filled with the Holy Spirit." Jesus did just that, and with this new hope, Gwen's has been a life of unbroken fellowship and service to Christ.

This leads us to the final point that the overwhelming message of the Bible as a whole is *the proclamation of the Redeemer*—the Lord from heaven! In Isaiah 59:20 we are assured, "The Redeemer will come to Zion!" So "the ransomed of the Lord will return. They will enter Zion with singing" (Isa. 51:11). The Redeemer of the world is Jesus, and He is Lord. So the coming of the Lord is for those who have come to the Lord. While most of the world awaits extermination, the believer awaits evacuation. The Christ who came 2,000 years ago to give His life for us on the cross is about to come again to give to us His crown of life forevermore. And only those who have believed on Him for salvation will rise to be with Him. One day Jesus asked His disciples, "When the Son of Man comes, will he find faith on the earth?" (Luke 18:8). Those who have faith will go with Him, at His coming. Those who don't, won't! For "Christ was sacrificed once to take away the sins of many people; and He will appear a second time, not to bear sin, but to bring salvation to those who are waiting for Him" (Heb. 9:28). So what is a Christian? A Christian, wrote Paul, is one who has "turned to God from idols to serve the living and true God, and to wait for his Son from heaven, whom he raised from the dead—Jesus, who rescues us from the coming wrath" (1 Thess. 1:9).

Psychology has long had a basic premise that life is predicated on one hub decision from which all other choices have their source. These other choices are like the spokes from a hub to the rim of a wheel. Life simply does not turn in balance unless that central decision has been made. God so constituted life that decision for Christ is the crucial choice, from which all others emanate.

On September 5, 1953, during a month-long crusade in Britain, I preached a message on the second coming of Christ. I was recently informed that in the packed crowd in the large tent that night was Constable Baird, his gracious wife, and three sons—Trevor, aged nineteen; Neville, fourteen; and Clifford, eight. At the end of the address and in response to the invitation of Jesus to do so, many people came forward and gave their lives to Christ. Among those confessing Christ were Constable and Mrs. Baird and a very decisive and determined Clifford. He was forever changed. On the way home that night, the father asked Neville and Trevor: "Should the Lord come again tonight, would you go to be with Him?" They didn't think they would. After a grave spiritual struggle, fourteen-year-old Neville made his response on September 22, and about a week later, Trevor did so. They were completely changed by giving their lives to Christ. Today Clifford is a psychologist and university instructor, living a life of enthusiastic service for Christ as is his brother Neville and their families in Wheaton, Illinois.

Trevor is minister of one of Canada's great churches, where it was my privilege to preach. He asked me to speak on the second coming of Christ, which I did, and that night, his son Stephen, nineteen, came forward to surrender his life to Jesus Christ. Trevor exclaimed: "That's three generations of my family: my parents, the three of us brothers, and now my son: all coming to Christ through your preaching the message of the second coming of Christ."

Friend, before you put this book down, ask yourself, "Am I a total believer in Christ as my personal Savior and eternal Lord? If Jesus were to come this moment, is my life entirely His?" If you have the slightest doubt, pray this prayer to Christ, who actually is on the doorstep of your life: "Lord Jesus Christ, come into my life in all Your fulness, cleanse me by Your shed blood from all of my sins, and fill me with Your Holy Spirit. Help me to read Your Word each day. And help me always to be ready for Your coming again by daily prayer and the determination to share my faith with others in the worship and fellowship of Your church. Thank you, Lord Jesus Christ. Amen!"

If you have made that decision for Christ, write me a letter, and I will be honored to send you some helpful literature. Write to: John Wesley White, Box 1000, Milliken, Ontario, Canada.